ASPECTS OF CONTEMPORARY PAINTING IN ALBERTA

VINCENT VARGA

GLENBOW MUSEUM ▪ CALGARY, ALBERTA

ASPECTS OF CONTEMPORARY PAINTING IN ALBERTA

an exhibition of contemporary painting organized by the Glenbow Museum with financial assistance from The Canada Council, the Calgary Region Arts Foundation, the Province of Alberta and The City of Calgary.

JULY 11, 1987 - AUGUST 30, 1987

Cover: Detail of *Picture of Friday* by David Verchomin

© Glenbow-Alberta Insitute, 1987
130-9 Avenue S.E.
Calgary, Alberta
Canada, T2G 0P3

ISBN 0-99224-68-7
Printed in Canada

Acknowledgements 6

Preface 7

Aspects of Contemporary Painting in Alberta 8

The Artists and Their Works 11

Notes 60

Bibliography 61

Artists' Biographies 64

Catalogue of the Exhibition 77

Index of Artists 80

Lenders to the Exhibition 81

CONTENTS

☐   This exhibition catalogue was made possible through the generous assistance and co-operation of many individuals and groups. While the following are selected for special mention, the many others too numerous to list here can be assured of my gratitude for their help.

Valuable context was provided through interviews with Helen Collinson, Ron Davey, Terry Fenton, Les Graff, Doug Haynes, Jetska Ironside, Tin Ng, Robert Sinclair, Norman Yates, and Liz Wylie, all of Edmonton; Ken Esler, John Hall, Harry Kiyooka, Doug Morton, Carroll Moppett, Ron Moppett, Peter Ohler, Peter Thielsen, and Nancy Tousley, all of Calgary; and Jeff Spalding of Lethbridge.

Special recognition is due to Karen Wonders, Leslie Dawn, and to members of the Glenbow staff for their valuable guidance, comments, and editorial assistance on the development of the manuscript, and to Elise L. Wittig for editorial input in the final copy.

David Bierk of Artspace gallery (Peterborough, Ontario), The Alberta Art Foundation (Edmonton), and The Canada Council Art Bank (Ottawa) deserve special mention for their help.

Sustained encouragement, advice and editorial comments were provided by Patricia Ainslie, and important details of the exhibition came from Christopher Jackson.

The Glenbow Board of Governors supported the project and enthusiastic co-operation came from the Glenbow's professional staff.

Finally, The Canada Council and the Calgary Region Arts Foundation contributed generous financial support for this exhibition and catalogue.

Vincent Varga
Associate Curator of Art
Glenbow Museum

☐ This exhibition entitled *Aspects of Contemporary Painting in Alberta* is the first survey in over a decade that examines the dynamic range of recent painting in the province. Since 1973 Alberta's larger public galleries have avoided compilations such as the *All Alberta* exhibitions which flourished between 1965 and 1973. While perhaps weak in defining a critical context, those exhibitions encouraged patrons to become familiar with contemporary art production by local artists. They also served as valuable opportunities for participating artists to be seen and evaluated by their peers. A contemporary overview of art-making in the province is, therefore, both timely and necessary.

With few exceptions, artists selected for *Aspects* received their formal art training in the province and/or are teaching at the Alberta College of Art, the University of Alberta, the University of Calgary, or the University of Lethbridge. These institutions have played a significant role in the development of a strong visual arts community in Alberta.

The focus of this catalogue essay is primarily on the development of the visual arts communities of Edmonton and Calgary from the early 1960s onward. By no means a definitive document or comprehensive study, it is intended however, to stimulate further, specific exploration into the richness of visual culture in Alberta. In fact, too little has been written on this important period in our cultural heritage. Consequently, although a comprehensive bibliography has been added, lively discussions and taped interviews provided the framework for this essay and exhibition.

PREFACE

Pluralism...reduces us to being another among others; it is not a recognition, but a reduction to difference to absolute indifference, equivalence, interchangeability. ...it is possible to speculate that what has toppled our claims to sovereignty is actually the realization that our culture is neither as homogeneous nor as monolithic as we once believed it to be.[1]

☐ Recent years have witnessed a dramatic expansion in painting in Alberta, characterized by a shift from regionalism to the forefront of what is frequently called the postmodern. Pluralism has, in fact, served as the driving force of contemporary creative production. Awareness and willingness to participate in the larger art scene, both nationally and internationally, has allowed artists in Alberta the freedom to explore, assimilate, and develop. This exhibition recognizes the diversity and range of present-day painting in showing the sheer dynamic talent and energy that is one of the province's greater natural resources.

To most Canadians, landscape images of Alberta and the prairies form the stereotypical notion of art production in this region. Indeed, Alberta artists perceive themselves as being relegated to the periphery of a national art history which has traditionally acted on the assumption that aesthetic quality is somehow mediated by geographical proximity to a recognized cultural centre. This notion of a paramount artistic centre with provincial hinterlands is being overturned by the new pluralism which denies the unquestioned authority of a particular region or city to dictate the aesthetic course which others must follow.

Alberta and the art produced in the province have explored a variety of stylistic approaches including photo realism, colourfield abstraction, minimalism, conceptual art, new image painting, and neo-expressionism. This receptiveness to various approaches has enabled artists in Alberta to come to terms with a personally appropriate style, identity, and relevance to place.

The general attitude of Alberta's visual arts community continues to be conditioned by its teaching institutions. A firm base from which future generations of artists will continue to draw has been developed during the past four decades. The teaching institutions deserve recognition for their continued and present role in fostering, encouraging, and training new talent: the Alberta College of Art (ACA), the University of Alberta (U of A), the University of Calgary (U of C), and the University of Lethbridge (U of L).[2] Not only do these institutions employ many professional artists, they serve as rallying points for students, faculty, and established artists where new approaches are taught, discussed, and critically examined.

The development of the visual arts community in Alberta during the past three decades parallels the transition from late modernism to what is generally known as post-modernism. Through the 1960s and 1970s Edmonton was a place of encouragement for modernist painters who explored the self-referential purity of form. This pursuit was supported by The Edmonton Art Gallery and reinforced by the Art Department at the University of Alberta. By contrast, the community in Calgary developed without an institutional, singular focus and its painting has tended to reflect concerns of content beyond medium. In Calgary, the ACA and the U of C focused on a pluralistic approach in which all avenues were explored.

To appreciate the accomplishments of the present, a brief review of the past three decades of growth and development is necessary. As elsewhere in the world, expansion and excitement characterized the 1960s nationally. The tone set by this frenetic expansion was positive and outward looking. This period witnessed the creation of universities that included liberal arts faculties alongside the sciences. During the late 1960s, the U of A (along with other Canadian universities) expanded exponentially, a factor related directly to the influx of baby boomers and the upscaling of the economy nationwide. The U of A had initiated its art program in 1946 under the direction of Henry George Glyde. From modest beginnings, the department rapidly expanded and gained momentum. Bachelor of Fine Arts programs were successfully implemented in Edmonton (1968) and Calgary (1969).

8

ASPECTS OF CONTEMPORARY PAINTING IN ALBERTA

The ACA underwent its own growing pains, moving into its present location in 1972, and gaining autonomy from the Southern Alberta Institute of Technology in 1985.[3]

With increased enrolments and expansion these institutions faced the difficulty of attracting suitable instructors. While the ACA frequently hired its own graduates, the universities were required to fill positions with graduate or equivalent level teaching staff. Due to a lack of qualified Canadians, artists who had earned graduate degrees in Great Britain and the United States often filled these positions, bringing with them a different cultural perspective.

Art-making during the post-World War Two years in Canada underwent a radical shift in orientation. Prior to this shift, the "Group of Seven" had established a regionalist Canadian wilderness - the northern Ontario wilderness - as the appropriate national image.[4] This prescriptive view began to be questioned by immigrant artists and Canadians familiar with the latest developments in international modernism. Significant to this era with respect to the Canadian context was the growing acceptance of international stylistic innovation. Generally, universities and colleges acted as conduits of information from the centres of the avant-garde. The modernist ideology was disseminated from New York, Paris, and London to the nascent teaching institutions. On the prairies, the Winnipeg School of Art introduced western Canadian artists to surrealism and abstraction in the years immediately following World War Two.[5]

The seminal workshops held at Emma Lake from 1955 to 1973 provided environments in which advanced painting was explored on the prairies.[6] The primary focus here was on self-critical painting practice and on the dialogue between artists and critics. The workshops afforded many prairie artists the sense of belonging to a larger movement. This need was born, in part, from a perception of isolation. That perception was tempered by the desire to participate in a dialogue that was beyond regional or nationalistic boundaries. The 1962 visit of noted American modernist art critic Clement Greenberg to Emma Lake was particularly significant. Greenberg successively championed the cause of abstract expressionism, post-painterly abstraction, and colourfield painting.[7] Several factors acting in unison established Regina and Edmonton as bastions of abstraction, with close ties to New York and Greenberg. Through its exhibitions, The Edmonton Art Gallery (The EAG) supported an international modernist approach.[8] For those artists who explored the Greenbergian approach, The EAG provided a critical forum where excellent modernist examples could be studied first hand.[9] During the 1970s and early 1980s, the gallery not only actively programmed American group and solo exhibitions of colourfield and post-painterly abstraction, it also purchased works by exhibiting artists.[10]

The influx of an international staff to the U of A Art Department found Edmonton a sympathetic environment in which to teach and paint. While the Art Department was not formally connected with The EAG, both provided fertile ground for students and others who wished to participate in this mainstream aesthetic discourse of the 1960s. According to Clement Greenberg, the mainstream revolved around appropriate content:

The history of avant-garde painting is that of a progressive surrender to the resistance of its medium; which resistance consists chiefly in the flat picture plane's denial of efforts to "hole through" it for realistic perspectival space. In making this surrender, painting not only got rid of imitation - and with it, "literature" - but also of realistic imitation's corollary confusion between painting and sculpture. ...most important of all, the picture plane itself grows shallower and shallower, flattening out and pressing together the fictive planes of depth until they meet as one upon the real material plane which is the actual surface of the canvas....[11]

In Edmonton as elsewhere, the connection to the mainstream became easier to maintain through increased access to New York and the ever-present barometer, the art magazines.

Through The EAG programs and the U of A curriculum, a support structure emerged that was especially conducive to the development of a strong community of abstract painters.[12] Of this group, many had received their art training at the ACA in Calgary but had moved to Edmonton where their work benefitted from peer interaction.

The diversification of styles recently established in Edmonton are not new in Calgary, where painting has been characterized by a variety of approaches since the 1960s. Variation and experimentation established Calgary as a centre of visual art throughout western Canada.

This tradition has been enhanced and maintained by the educational institutions in concert with Calgary's three major galleries: the Glenbow Museum, the Nickle Arts Museum, and the Alberta College of Art Gallery. These exhibition spaces have provided regional, national, and international programming that has informed the community. Smaller yet equally important spaces, such as Off Centre Centre and the Muttart Gallery, have also made significant contributions to the development of painting in the city.[13] While a high degree of technical facility and craftsmanship is evident in Calgary, the content is not restricted to purely formal concerns. Representation, narrative, metaphor, and other literary associations co-exist with late modernist approaches.

Within the diversity of Calgary's visual arts community, problems in late modernism are explored by Bruce O'Neil, Gerald Hushlak, and William MacDonnell. As a point of departure, both MacDonnell and Hushlak draw on aesthetic conventions established by formal modernist painting. John Hall, Chris Cran, and John Brocke represent the growing number of realist painters in Calgary who share the same style, although their approaches vary considerably.

Community colleges and universities established in communities such as Lethbridge, Red Deer, Medicine Hat, and Grand Prairie, service the growing educational needs of these smaller cities. Lethbridge, the largest of these centres is home to a modestly scaled university which houses an active art gallery that has developed a superlative collection of international, contemporary prints. Through both the U of L gallery and the Southern Alberta Art Gallery, regional and national art is actively included in their programs.

Painters have formed the core of the visual arts community in Alberta and the discipline has occupied a central role in the curriculum of the colleges and universities. The preceding three decades have witnessed a growing sense of self-confidence among the painters of the province. Most of the artists featured in *Aspects* have exhibited nationally and internationally, lending validity to the quality of the teaching institutions and to the vibrancy of the visual arts community of Alberta.

The selection of artists for this exhibition neither reaffirms a linear progression of development nor presents a chronology of senior artists followed by the younger avant-garde. Rather, it adopts a pluralistic vision that reflects the development of painting in Alberta.

What is evident from these works is that the preceding decades have fostered an increased awareness of place within the national and international spheres of art. These paintings offer an amalgam of approaches that at times is harmonious and at others dissonant. By drawing this selection together *Aspects of Contemporary Painting in Alberta* does not authorize a particular direction but celebrates the unique, individual nature of the creative sensibilities of these committed artists. ■

THE ARTISTS AND THEIR WORKS

☐   Rather than working horizontally, Giuseppe Albi has chosen to confront the canvas vertically, on an easel. His method relies on the integration of the subconsciously inspired, spontaneous approach of automatic drawing and the evocative, chromatic potential of post-painterly abstraction. For Albi, these ethereal images serve as referents to personal psychological states. Evocative, atmospheric paintings are achieved through the use of a technique in which Albi builds up thin, transparent layers of pigmented gel. The creation of a relatively smooth surface devoid of articulation or physical depth focuses the viewer's attention on the emotive qualities of colour and amorphous form. To enforce viewer identification even further with the image, Albi uses a vertical format in collaboration with atmospheric space to produce rich, reflective, psychological portraits.

GIUSEPPE ALBI

BERG
acrylic on canvas, 1986, (cat. no. 2)

Eva Diener had studied in Europe and Australia before settling in Edmonton. She has recently adopted an approach that is informed by her previous abstract work, yet derives impetus from the bravura of German or Italian neo-expressionism. Rather than using painting as a self-referential aesthetic, Diener allows content and subject matter to invade her work. Diener's evocative paintings convey the fundamental struggles of human existence caught in moments of metaphysical crisis. In a series of works entitled *Transit*, Diener explores, through her poignant images, the intensity of living, psychic existential alienation, and the authenticity of experience in images drawn from the collective psyche. This concern for the human condition is enlarged upon in her recent *Toxic* paintings. Diener grapples with the very real and topical problems of environmental pollution, whether it be through nuclear or chemical disaster. *Toxic # 10* (1986) and *Toxic # 12* (1987) are riveting emotional images of the consuming nature of this creeping menace. Diener's paintings are heartfelt reflections of works protesting global environmental annihilation.

EVA DIENER

Toxic # 12
acrylic on canvas, 1987, (cat. no. 10)

☐   Doug Haynes attended the ACA in the late 1950s and moved to Edmonton in the early 1960s when the community of modernist painters was small and the task large. His work (as with most of the abstract painters in this exhibition) derives its impetus from the formalist aesthetic as described by Clement Greenberg.

Artists such as Haynes, Robert Scott, Terrence Keller, and Albi share a common interest in surface; variation is achieved by an approach adopted to the application of pigment. The sculptural quality of the surface is generally achieved through the use of acrylic paints, either thinned to watercolour consistency and soaked into unsized canvas, or mixed with transparent gels applied to unstretched canvas (generally on the floor) with scrapers, trowels, and other similar tools. Such paintings are often reworked several times. Each successive layer adds density and dimension to the surface. Although colour within Haynes' works tends to be limited to a narrow range, it is directly linked to the texture and gesture, and embodies the expressive element of the work.

Haynes' most recent work seeks to reinvestigate cubism from the perspective of the 1980s. In *Apple Swing* (1986) and *Diego's Table* (1986), Haynes has fractured the surface by applying pigmented gel in fragmented arcs, wedges, and planes. A familiar cubist device, the guitar, emerges from these configurations as a sign, yet never becomes representational, as stress on the pigment's physical tactility, transparency, and opacity locks the image into its material base.

DOUG HAYNES

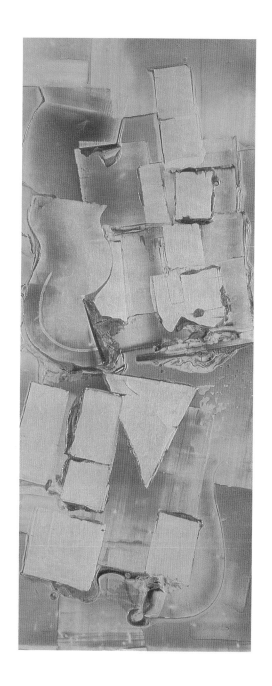

Apple Swing
acrylic on canvas, 1986, (cat. no. 18)

☐   Terrence Keller has adopted a method of producing pictures that relies on the heavy buildup of pigmented gel. Keller works on the floor on unstretched canvas where gel is laid down on the surface and then trowelled with a variety of scrapers. Depending on the viscosity of the medium, the surface assumes a plastic sheen on the one extreme, and a complexion of sun-baked earth on the other. Once he has built up an overall background through successive layering, Keller tends to complete the work with a "big move." This gestural mark (or marks) tends to span the width of the canvas, as in *Med Hat* (1985-86) where the surfaces depend on subtle variations in tone and chroma. Although his palette leans toward earth tones in *Round Midnight* (1987), an iridescent mauve brings the surface to life. Through an effective juxtaposition of heavy, weighty surface and ethereal colour, the canvas seems to hover outward from the wall. When a deeply cracked surface painted in neutral earth tones is combined with a horizontal format, Keller's work assumes landscape associations. Through the gestural manipulation of a thickly gelled surface, Keller draws attention to the plastic, sculptural qualities of the medium.

TERRENCE KELLER

Hat Med
acrylic and gel on canvas, 1985-86, (cat. no. 22)

☐   Robert Scott attended the ACA but moved to Edmonton soon after he graduated in 1969. Utilizing techniques associated with late post-painterly abstraction, and specifically Jules Olitski, Scott applies successive layers of paint with a spray gun. This technique yields a thick carpet of pigment which he then works with his fingers, leaving trails of gestural imprints. Eliminating the bristle brush and making direct contact with the medium allows the gesture to embody the expressive character of the picture.

ROBERT SCOTT

Graphite Whisper
acrylic on canvas, 1986, (cat. no. 38)

☐ Suzanne Spiegel-Bell of Edmonton has continued to paint in an abstract manner since her graduation from the U of A in 1983. While the majority of her peers are concerned with rich surfaces and gesture, Spiegel-Bell's large canvases are a synthesis of abstract styles, revolving around the expressive quality of colour and the tension of intersecting geometric forms. Her paintings deny texture, allowing the canvas to resonate through an emotional character associated with muted colour relationships and compositional configurations. The work often hinges on the juxtaposition of a single, diminutive form in relation to a large field. The images that Spiegel-Bell constructs can be viewed as an identification of self within a larger, delineated landscape.

SUZANNE SPIEGEL-BELL

C Player
acrylic on canvas, 1986-87, (cat. no. 42)

☐ David Verchomin attended the U of A following which he earned a graduate degree at the University of Maryland in 1984. While there, Verchomin was exposed to new image painting, an approach that reconciled modernist notions of surface and paint with representational, figurative imagery. Wit and irony characterize his approach.

In *Window Pie # 1* (1986) Verchomin presents a view of a yellow wedge shape that is obscured by an internal pink frame. This device is painted with broad strokes that reinforce the flat nature of the support. The apparent planar surface, however, is then disturbed by a window punched through the centre of the canvas. On what appears to be a receding plane, the wedge of pie forms the horizon to a spacious powder-blue sky.

In *Picture of Friday* (1986) the artist uses a portrait of a dog perched on a table as a compositional device to provide access to the painting. Again, a painted, internal frame isolates the object and reiterates the flat nature of the canvas. Verchomin's vigorous drawing and brushwork deny the creation of an illusory space. A limited perspectival zone exists through the use of a two-dimensional schematic representation of a hemisphere over the dog's head. This indication of volume is restated twice: once in a blue elliptical plane that intersects the dog at the shoulders, and then by the table surface on which the animal sits.

DAVID VERCHOMIN

Picture of Friday
oil on canvas, 1986, (cat. no. 44)

Jack Anderson appropriates images from the past without ignoring the significance of the original. These sophisticated, sensitive works explore the layered (ideological and iconographic) character of a single object and how cultures separated by geography and time provide varied interpretations. In *The Conversation* (1985) and *Growling at the Moon* (1985), Anderson presents an archaeology of aesthetic forms.

In a contemporary critical environment that refutes the notion of an enduring object, Anderson presents a scenario that suspends this belief, if only for a moment. He adopts a form that has little to do with anxiety-ridden, contemporary society or art practice. These works receive impetus from concepts of classical beauty and visual perception, as embodied in the shape of the amphora.

The amphora is introduced into a discourse that draws upon conceptual associations contained in classical aesthetics - notions of ideal form that fuse object and symbol into a single entity. In *The Conversation* Anderson introduces the amphora motif by illustrating the paradigm of simultaneous meaning. Two heads in profile, facing one another form an amphora while two figures incised into the negative space engage in the strategic game of chess. This highly ornate surface and compelling image alludes to Marcel Duchamp, conceptual artist and chess master.

In *Growling at the Moon* Anderson associates self with the amphora by introducing it into a domestic, architectural interior. This Hegelian metaphor for mental inwardness corresponds to the interior of the building; thus, by extension, the amphora becomes the focus of reflection. Painted on a black ground, forest green, velvety purple, and iridescent blue form the palette of this dream-like canvas. Through a window, the silvery light of the moon penetrates the darkened bedroom. Moonlight strikes the opposite wall, cleaving a chair, table, and amphora in half. At the foot of the bed, a rug with an image of a growling animal looks out at the moon.

By placing the amphora in a domestic environment, Anderson alludes to notions of sanctuary, resting places, and the familiar. Through the selection of the amphora motif, he illustrates the multiplicity of meaning within visual and object culture. By isolating the amphora from its art historical past and justifying its personal relevance, Anderson has reintroduced the form as if it were inherently enduring, yet contemporary.

JACK ANDERSON

Growling at the Moon
acrylic on canvas, 1985 (cat. no. 4)

Questioning the known image is at the core of John Brocke's exploration of realistic image-making. Brocke is concerned with the mystical possibilities embodied in the use of realistic imagery. He compiles photographs of individuals, objects, and physical relationships, and edits them into a single image that corresponds to a moment of intense personal revelation. The works are highly charged scenes where identification is established with an individual in an unlikely situation. Brocke has developed a realist approach derived from the neo-impressionist technique of brief, minute, individual brush marks that, in unison, create an image. Through a sophisticated approach to optical colour-mixing, which is achieved through layering of the fields of marks, Brocke produces images that resonate with life.

In *Barb/Barbaros* (1985) Brocke presents a scene pervaded by a sense of déjà vu. This "vision" takes place outside the Muttart Art Gallery in Central Park, Calgary. Psychological tension is established between the viewer and the young female figure placed at the centre of the image. Flanking the central figure on the left, a man walks his dog while on the right, a brown bear nonchalantly ambles out of the frame. Neither human nor beast seem aware of the other, yet a tension resounds across the scintillating surface of the canvas. Electrified by the outward gaze of the girl, the painting assumes a character beyond snapshot portraiture. By structuring the canvas symmetrically Brocke imbues the work with a significance that borders on the religious, not unlike an icon.

JOHN BROCKE

Barb/Barbaros
oil on canvas, 1985, (cat. no. 5)

Chris Cran's approach to realism hinges on a critical understanding of cinematic and spectacular moments. *Self Portrait Watching A Man About to Shoot Himself in the Foot* (1985) creates a carefully posed, theatrical tableau based on this cliché. Cran transcends its banality and gives it new significance by posing himself in the foreground waiting in suspense for the discharge of the rifle. Here, Cran questions any voyeuristic relationship to his images. He seeks the viewer's active involvement in these preconceived scenarios, through a vicarious identification with the artist. In *Portrait of Me as Max Beckman* (1986) Cran turns this technique around by humorously identifying himself with a known art historical figure where the dividing lines between identity and fiction, viewer and viewed, are subtly effaced.

30

CHRIS CRAN

Self Portrait Watching a Man About to Shoot Himself in the Foot
oil on canvas, 1985, (cat. no. 7)

☐ For the past three to four years, Alan Dunning has explored the relationship between the drawn image and its perception. In his large, wall-sized panoramas, Dunning utilizes gallery spaces as if they were one large, continuous sheet of paper. The notion of real space and drawn space often becomes confused through the placement of elements on the floor and adjoining walls.

Dunning's recent work expands on the notion of perception as not only a sensory phenomenon but an interactive process between memory and the eye. In *Unfinished Business - Seaside* (1986-87) Dunning shifts from butcher paper to canvas tarpaulin. His concern for the expressive potential of the support is retained in this work. The folds, weave, and seams of the tarpaulin are accented through the application of charcoal and paint. Cryptic representations of ocean, sky, field, book, and flesh conjured from memory are littered across the canvas with no apparent structure emerging to unify the narrative; yet, a subtle logic has been imposed through the process of production. For each signifier, the artist makes a stencil or composite of stencils and it is this that becomes an ordering principle for this complex, multi-layered work. While the stencil defines the sign, the narrative remains elusive due to unfamiliar vocabulary. Dunning, through this approach to notions of memory, vocabulary, and narrative, questions the process by which objects and concepts are articulated and how meaning is created.

ALAN DUNNING

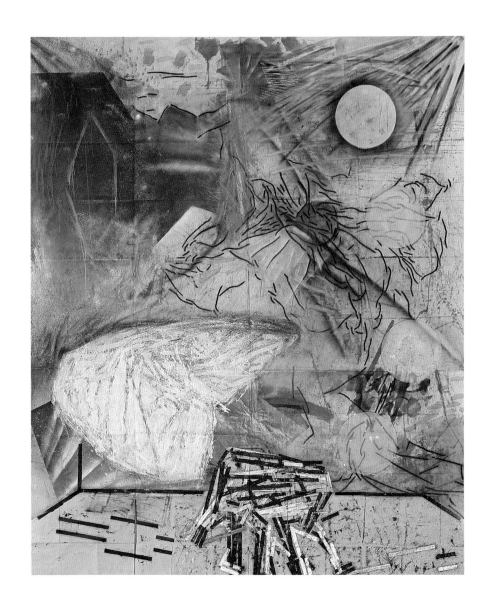

Unfinished Business - Seaside
mixed media, 1986-87 (cat. no. 11)

☐ The structuring of space, whether it be physical or illusionistic, is the predominant direction that Wayne Giles pursues in his painting. Through wall-mounted, painted, relief constructions, Giles began to explore sculptural space in the 1980s. Using found and cut plywood, he built up these images and painted them to enhance depth or deny it. His recent work continues this direction of image formation and construction with emphasis on illusionistic space. This return to the flat, stretched canvas also coincides with Giles' reintroduction of representational and figurative associations.

In *Race* (1986) and *No Picnic* (1986), the notion of formation and construction are presented as ambiguous, visual narratives. Caught in the state of flux, these images document a fictitious "Big Bang." The dynamic character of the image hinges on the paradox between existing geometric solids, emerging organic forms, and the vibrating vortex. On the one hand, if the notion of implosion were adopted, then the vortex would assume a malevolent character, consuming all. On the other hand, the unbridled kinetic energy of the vortex represents the process of formation.

The viewer is implicated as a witness to this transformation process. A cartoon-like head peers into the viewer's space with a look of disbelief, as if the explanation exists outside the space defined by the canvas. The viewer is placed in the position of extrapolating the end result. By leaving the image in a dynamic state, caught between chaos or coherence, Giles presents images that hang precariously on the edge of resolution.

WAYNE GILES

No Picnic
acrylic on canvas, 1986, (cat. no. 13)

☐ John Hall attended the ACA in the early 1960s when abstract expressionism was the predominant style. After graduating he turned to realism which he felt had greater relevance to his own thought process. Hall's paintings characteristically contain an eclectic array of "objects" — popular culture artifacts that he arranges and paints through the aid of photography. Although the resulting images resemble large studio photographs, the selection of kitsch souvenirs (vessels of memory?), done with startling intensity of colour and light, is transformed into iconic portraits that question the value and meaning of objects.

Arlene (1986) and *Indigo* (1986) illustrate two aspects of Hall's work. While the two canvases are identical stylistically and share compositional conventions, the impact of *Arlene* tends toward the cerebral, while *Indigo* is overwhelmingly visceral. In *Arlene*, personal, borrowed objects are represented in a layered tableau. The painting abounds with second- or third-generation facsimiles of appropriated imagery, questioning the notion of the original, and the sense of illusory reality.

In *Indigo* Hall has constructed an image that lies in deep shadow with piercing light illuminating selected objects. The theatricality of the tableau is heightened by a dazzling sunset in the background. The objects of attention are a flower, a high-heeled shoe, a necklace and other paraphernalia. This piece transcends the materialism inherent in work like *Arlene*. Through a synthesis of compositional structure, selection of objects, and theatrical lighting, Hall has constructed a loaded, mesmerizing, and fetishistic painting that evokes the power of religious icons.

36

JOHN HALL

Indigo
acrylic on canvas, 1986, (cat. no. 16)

For the past several years, Joice Hall has painted the male figure, and images she appropriates from fashion magazines provide the point of departure. Although highly nuanced, the figures are denied individuality through an approach that promotes the stereotypical. The male form becomes a "blow-up" doll presented in a number of posed situations.

During a recent stay at the Banff Centre, Hall devoted her energies to painting the local environs. This shift in subject matter allowed her to apply this reductive approach to the landscape. *Floating* (1985-86) is a sixteen-panel painting that incorporates both figurative orientation and landscape. Photographs taken from the top of Sulphur Mountain, outside of Banff, provide the background for the tumbling human form. Like the Greek god Helios, this free-floating male form is caught, in freeze-frame, gently rising and falling over the serene Banff landscape. Hall's juxtaposition of cool, silvery grey in the figures with the warm earth tones of the landscape create an aura of ethereality.

JOICE HALL

Floating
(panels 11, 12, 13, 14), oil on canvas, 1985-86, (cat. no. 17)

□   Gerald Hushlak's approach is based both in the area of
      colourfield abstraction and his continued research into
the production of images through the use of computers. Hushlak uses the computer in much the same way as another artist
would use a pencil to produce preliminary sketches. While the
computer functions as a tool on one level, it also allows the artist
to distance himself from the aesthetics of production. As a sur-
rogate memory, the computer can store multiple variations of
an image serving as a repository of visual information.

The paintings that develop are not merely representations of
computer- generated images. The interface between technology and the canvas occurs more in a metaphorical sense as a
layering of processed information. For example, in *I asked for
horse shoes they gave me wings. Now I'm going to fly!* (1986-
87), Hushlak uses an image of a running horse as a formal
compositional device presented in two contrasting ways. In the
far right panel of the painting, a schematic, winged horse is dis-
cernible in the heavily built-up surface. Illusory space is denied
through the articulation of the surface. By creating overloaded
surfaces, Hushlak draws attention to physical characteristics of
the paint and reinforces the planar nature of the support.

The centre panel is calm by comparison. On a piece of found
trucking tarpaulin, Hushlak delineates the head and withers of
a horse with brief, yellow brushstrokes. Once again, the animal
image serves as a compositional device to lure the viewer. The
unprimed tarpaulin assumes a skin-like character drawing attention to the support.

In the left panel Hushlak combines the two approaches presented in the centre and right panels. Through the juxtaposition
of densely articulated painted space and the skin-like surface,
Hushlak vibrantly echoes the modernist paradigm.

CALGARY

GERALD HUSHLAK

I asked for horse shoes, they gave me wings. Now I'm going to fly!
oil on canvas (four modules), 1986-87, (cat. no. 21)

Since 1984 Don Kottmann has embarked on a visual odyssey that examines the human psyche through the time-honoured tradition of portraiture. While the theme is conventional, Kottmann adopts a neo-expressionist approach that integrates psychological and emotional interpretation with vibrant colour, gestural marks, and loose brushwork.

The two group portraits featured in the exhibition, *Last Judgement* (1986) and *Beacon Tandava* (1986), are scenes drawn from the popular culture of the tavern. In these group portraits Kottmann delves into the collective psyche of the macho, beer-garden mentality. Not only are copious amounts of beer visible, but Kottmann's vision reasserts the notion of debauchery, consumption, and lust. Human figures are depicted with flurries of vibrant, contrasting colour giving the impression of borderline nausea. Bodies are lost in the pea-soup smoke, with the occasional appendage emerging from the smog. Booze, smoke, and bleary eyes serve as the context for the main event - the stripper.

42

In *Last Judgement* the naked female figure emerges like a genie from a glass of beer held by a patron. A kneeling stripper is presented in *Beacon Tandava* alongside a schematic representation of an eastern dancing goddess - an hallucination? For both these works, Kottmann has focused attention on the strippers by rendering the majority of their bodies as solid areas of colour, in contrast to his fragmented treatment of the audience. As if to gauge the reality of the situation, or as a gesture - to touch the goddess - an extended hand is painted in personalizing the drama to the viewer as participant in this spectacle. Kottmann continues to develop his bold, expressive approach in the paint handling as well as in his exploration of the fascinating realm of individual and group psyche.

DON KOTTMANN

Beacon Tandava
acrylic on canvas, 1986, (cat. no. 25)

☐ In his paintings, William MacDonnell reconciles the shift from the modernist notion of self-referentiality with the reintroduction of content and image. *Untitled* (1983) is the schematic representation of two mirrored chairs sharing a central axis and extending to the edges. The thick application of paint and drawn forms produce a highly tactile surface that allows for a formal reading. In MacDonnell's painting:

...the image represents the successful reconciliation of figure and ground, while preserving the integrity of the picture plane. It narrowly escapes this modernist cliché, however, by coyly suggesting that both chairs and canvas serve as supports and are thus linguistically as well as visually interchangeable.[15]

MacDonnell continues the debate surrounding flat surface, while reintroducing the notion of image and content. In *Untitled* (1986) a stylized horse is caught running across the surface of a dark expanse. This same surface serves as a field for the short marks that uniformly cover the painting. MacDonnell again creates a situation of perceptual and conceptual interchangeability. In this case, the surface of the canvas exists as a surface for both the horse and marks to traverse.

44

WILLIAM MACDONNELL

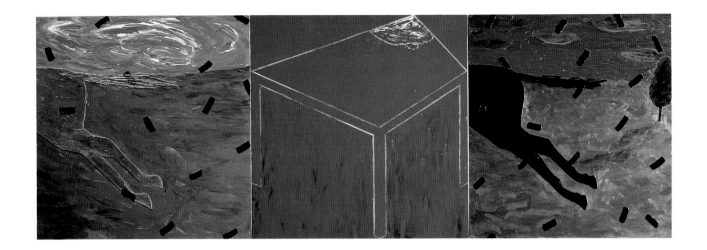

Untitled
oil on canvas, 1986, (cat. no. 29)

To Carroll Moppett, painting is a way of synthesizing memories of significant moments drawn from personal experience. The juxtaposition of diverse images and layering of meanings is achieved through collage. This stylistic device provides a vocabulary by which the canvas is unified.

In *Biography, Autobiography: I Am I Not Any Longer When I See* (1985), Moppett presents a large horizontal drawing, a personal diary of her voyage of discovery through art-making. In reference to Moppett's work, John Bentley Mays pointed out that many contemporary painters "often do much rethinking about the heritage of Western painting, its forms and manners and techniques."[16]

A traditional landscape on the left progresses through a series of cubist metamorphoses and emerges on the right as a view into a dark, mysterious garden of amorphous forms. The autobiographic work not only serves as a personal record, but in many ways is an apt metaphor for the development and acceptance of modernism in the visual arts community of Alberta.

During the summer of 1985 Moppett spent three weeks in Yugoslavia as a visiting artist. While there she became acutely aware of the electrifying nature of culture shock. To mediate the experience of a stopover in Belgrade (Beograd), Moppett conceived of and painted a series of four canvases entitled *Like Trying to See Beograd* (1985). In these canvases, a collision of cultures takes place. According to *Calgary Herald* critic Nancy Tousley, aspects of Islamic, Indian, Byzantine, and Albertan culture form a cross-cultural amalgam:

Their sources reveal her abiding interest in how other cultures manifest their beliefs in visual things.[17]

In *Beograd*, a pitcher brimming with water serves as a metaphorical introduction to the rich world of an alien culture. An ornate fence acts as a barrier, restricting access yet allowing a cursory view. A schematic representation of an ornate force separates the foreground from the various architectural and landscape views. This contemplative recollection by Moppett succinctly addresses the notion of a stranger in a strange land and how culture and memory mediate experience.

CARROLL MOPPETT

Biography, Autobiography: I am I Not Any Longer When I See
charcoal on canvas, 1985, (cat. no. 31)

Dream-like scenes occupied by enigmatic visual signs and rich passages of paint characterize Ron Moppett's evocative and complex painting. In *Indian Red/Portrait/Buffalo* (1983) Moppett creates a dynamic tension between the allusive quality of the textured, painted surface and the flat schematic representations of personal signs. References to regional, indigenous native cultures are suggested in both the title and his choice of landscape and buffalo.

In the right-hand panel of this diptych, a schematic representation of a chair serves as a metaphor for contemplative study or a seat of knowledge. Joining the two panels, a cruciform of unpainted wood functions as a compositional device and as an abstracted ideological referent - a crucifix as well as a simplified representation of an airplane.

According to Nancy Tousley:

**Meanings turn on dualities such as these, and
formal flip flops between the abstract
and representational elements, but what one
finally grasps arrives like a feeling,
something intuited rather than known.**[14]

In *Paris* (1986) Moppett continues to explore notions associated with the duality of meaning and the canvas resonates with clairvoyant vision. The multitude of personal symbols denies a complete, simultaneous reading. Moppett uses the selective nature of memory as a device to integrate both interpreted information and intuited experience. Enlarged stencils of images appropriated from diverse sources such as consumer catalogues and art history texts illustrate one layer of this complex of meaning.

The left-hand panel contains a western Canadian landscape as opposed to a symbolic representation. This sense of nature as a defined geographical site is jostled by the word "Paris" in the bottom right corner that, according to the artist, also refers to the mythological persona. A painted cut-out of a man at work in the landscape along with the cabin reinforces the notion of physical, environmental space.

The centre panel, an interior scene appropriated from a 16th century painting by Veronese, refers to the notion of interior architectural space, hence, the arena of culture.

The final panel presents images of a schematic glowing, yellow-orange fire on a black field, a chair and two large floating pearls. These objects represent notions of personal interior spaces, seats of knowledge, pearls of wisdom, and creative fires. This complex montage of images and symbols necessitates a multi-textual reading that invites the viewer to interpret through personal association and memory.

RON MOPPETT

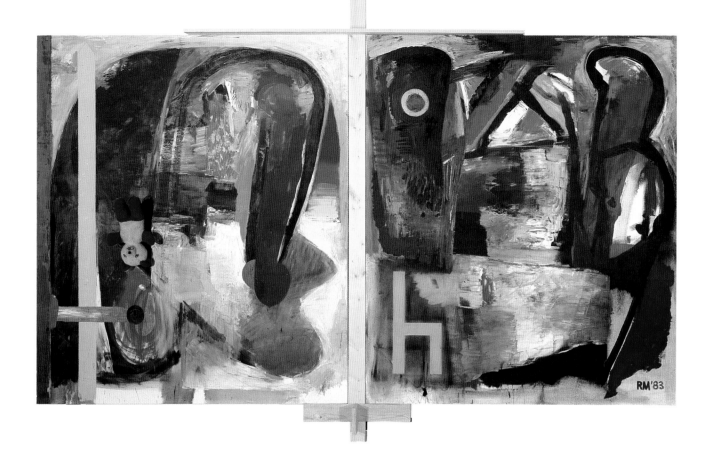

Indian Red/Portrait/Buffalo
oil on canvas, teddy bear, wood, 1983, (cat. no. 33)

☐ Bruce O'Neil attended the ACA during the 1960s and recently has taught at both the U of C and the ACA. He has continued to explore and expand the rich terrain of post-painterly abstraction. While many of his counterparts in Edmonton chose to build up tactile surfaces, O'Neil has adopted an alternative approach. Rather than creating depth through articulation of layers of pigmented gel, he has adopted a watercolour technique. Large areas of the canvas are stained with thinned acrylic medium, allowing the paint to bleed into the support, as in *Silver Shift* (1980-84). Paint of varying viscosity applied on top of the ground punctuates the surface. Through the juxtaposition of large areas of stained canvas and gestural marks, O'Neil establishes figure/ground relationships that activate the image. Flurries of turquoise, yellow, and white on a cool green ground bring *Tenak* (1986) to a dynamic state. The energy is amplified by the two flying wedges that contribute to the illusion of depth.

O'Neil tempts the viewer's sense of recognition in *Silver Shift*. A partially formed trough floats in an ethereal, primordial sea of blues and greens. Not only can this be read as a schematic representation of a conduit, but it also appears to be poised on the brink of assuming a concrete identity. O'Neil continues to explore avenues of abstraction that remain self-referential while infusing notions of image and content.

CALGARY

BRUCE O'NEIL

Tenak
acrylic on canvas, 1986, (cat. no. 34)

□ Mary Scott's paintings address social issues, including access to power, feminism, and sexuality. They are, however, more seductive than rhetorical in nature and embody a complex relationship between image and text, originality and appropriation, and ultimately, the language and meaning of desire. In both *Untitled (Stealers!)* (1986) and *Untitled (quoting L. Irigaray, R. Barthes; image - Jean Genet, 1953)* (1986), Scott overlays a vague, shadowy image drawn from popular media with a text extracted from a related source. The paint quality is luxurious, disarming, and alluring, yet the content takes on a harder edge that goes beyond mere delectation of surface.

Although knowledge of her specific sources is, as the titles imply, not necessary to gain access to these works, the image/text juxtaposition provides clues to introduce the viewer to a broader discourse embedded in a meta-textual reading. According to Bradley and Lemiroff, in Scott's work a complex text emerges:

...one that is elliptical and elusive, two-faced, open yet entangled, seductive yet resistant. Nor is this a text in which one voice alone speaks or where one single meaning must be read. Scott, like the feminist writers she quotes, wishes to release the polysemous potential of language from the bonds of a linear, logocentric discourse.... The motif that recurs throughout Scott's work in both the writing and the imagery - which she has taken from soft-core and art-world pornography as well as from art history — is that of the body. The reclaiming of the female body by making audible her speech is a central part of Scott's project.[18]

MARY SCOTT

Untitled (quoting L. Irigaray, R. Barthes; image - Jean Genet 1953)
mixed media, 1986, (cat. no. 36)

□   John Will, an expatriate American, often approaches life in Calgary with a witty sense of humour. During the 1970s he focused attention on issues of regionalism and nationalism as expressions of society's sense of place. Appropriated images from popular culture and the world of high art have become Will's vehicles for tongue-in-cheek illustrations of North American culture.

The works featured here continue this satirical and ironic amalgam of popular and fine art whereby bumper stickers are the initial impetus for the painting. For North American culture, the bumper sticker acts as a barometer for gauging popular attitudes and offering insights into the collective psyche. Will appropriates these statements and using his sophisticated wit, modifies them to yield humorous, succinct and multi-layered indictments against modern society. Two untitled works (1983; 1985) are components of a continuing series of images in an identical format. Predominance is lent to the bumper sticker by its central placement on the canvas. Adjacent polaroid photographs are glued and isolated on large painted fields. For example, in *Untitled* (1985) the emblematic text is flanked by two illustrious Americans, Richard Nixon and Andy Warhol, whose polaroid photographs (taken by Will) are fixed to a painted background of four American flags. Even this image is all too familiar, as Will makes an oblique reference to Jasper Johns' flag series of the 1950s. Through the juxtaposition of bumper stickers, polaroids, and painting, Will seems to propose that Nixon and Warhol be added to the constellation of stars as exemplary Americans. This proposition questions how North American culture grants star status.

JOHN WILL

Untitled
oil on canvas, 1985, (cat. no. 46)

☐   Billy McCarroll uses appropriated images from Sam Snead's *Natural Golf* in *Full Follow Through* (1986) and The *Square Stance* (1986). These paintings are cropped, edited, and enlarged versions of single pages of this self-help manual for golfers. Although the images have a direct affinity with Pop Art, they are rendered in an amalgam of modernist styles. While the application of oil and oil stick on canvas yields rich, colourful, textural surfaces, the real depth of McCarroll's work lies in its ironic metaphors. As Peter White observes:

McCarroll's best device, however, is probably golf. As a game whose angst is out of all proportion to its worldly importance, golf offers a continuous humorous counterpoint to the inflated seriousness of much recent art.... compared to art, at least according to the terms of this particular discourse, golf is utterly without pretense, or, apparently, redeeming social worth. Which is precisely the point.[20]

McCarroll has provocatively loaded a vehicle drawn from popular culture to comment on both the discourse of high art and on the crises presented in society's everyday world.

As alluded to in Snead's *Natural Golf*, McCarroll extends the metaphor further by implying that the only successful approach is the honest, natural one; once again, another double-edged metaphor equally fitting for any endeavour whether it be art, life, or golf.

BILLY McCARROLL

The Square Stance
oil on canvas, 1986, (cat. no. 29)

☐   In *NightFall* (1984) and *Dark Source: Threshold* (1987), Jeffrey Spalding presents paintings that are a departure from the earlier systemic and process works. In these recent paintings, the narrative metaphorical content is the vehicle for meaning, rather than signification arising from the material process. These operatic works lack the heavy build-up of acrylic gels typical of earlier paintings but rely on the invocation of atmosphere through subtle tonal shifts. The canvases seem to radiate an iridescent light generated from within, and the metaphoric image serves as the source of inspiration.

In *NightFall* Spalding presents a nocturnal view in which the luminous green wedge of Niagara Falls emerges veiled in evocative passages of misty greys and cool greens. This painting suggests a contemporary reappraisal of notions affiliated with the 19th century romantic landscape painting.

The painting stands as a metaphor for the subjugation of nature to man's industrial and military technocracy. Niagara Falls no longer has the power to inspire awe in light of the destructive potential of a single nuclear device. The painting brings us to the precipice of a new dark age.[19]

Dark Source: Threshold continues this symbolic and metaphoric investigation into man's relationship to nature. In the midst of a velvety, nocturnal, blackness, a wedge of penetrating light defines a silvery, mountain waterfall and a bottomless pool. In the upper pool a greenish mist obscures the source of the falls. The painting serves as a metaphor illustrating the paradox of the creative potential of the psyche in opposition to the consuming nature of the process.

58

LETHBRIDGE   JEFFREY SPALDING

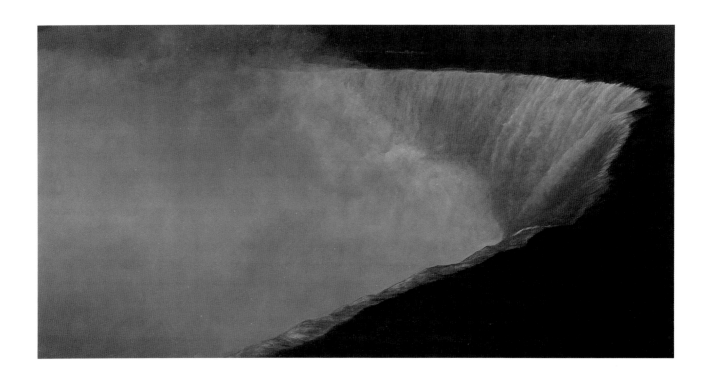

Nightfall
oil on canvas, 1984-85, (cat. no. 40)

1. Craig Owens, "The Discourse of Others: Feminists and Postmodernism," *The Anti-Aesthetic: Essays on Postmodern Culture* (Port Townsend, WA: Bay Press, 1983), p. 58

2. The Banff School of Fine Arts serves as an important catalyst for artists in Alberta and as a teaching institution cannot be overlooked, but due to its policy of rotating, changing faculty, it was not possible to single out individuals whose presence created an impact equal to those at other institutions. The early history of art-making in Alberta has been dealt with in detail in a number of books, articles, and exhibitions catalogues, some of which are listed in the bibliography.

3. For a brief history of the ACA, see Val Greenfield, "Introduction", *A Measure of Success: Graduates of the Alberta College of Art 1963-1984* (Calgary: Alberta College of Art, 1985), pp.4-8.

4. Peter Mellen, *The Group of Seven* (Toronto: McClelland & Stewart Ltd., 1970).

5. For an overview of the development of modernism on the prairies, see Christopher Varley, *Winnipeg West: Painting and Sculpture in Western Canada* 1945-1970 (Edmonton: The Edmonton Art Gallery, 1983).

6. Refer to the bibliography for selected articles and catalogues that discuss the significance of Emma Lake and its role in nurturing modernism on the prairies.

7. Clement Greenberg, "Post-painterly Abstraction," *Art International* 8 (Summer 1964).

8. Programming at The EAG during the 1970s exposed local artists to selected exhibitions, for example: The *Non-Figurative Artists' Association of Montreal* (1985); *American Accents* (1984); *Walter Darby Bannard: Recent Painting* (1983); *Jules Olitski: Paintings of the 70s* (1979); *Jack Bush: A Retrospective* (1977); *Canada x Ten! Abstract Paintings by Ten Canadian Artists* (1974); *Masters of the Sixties* (1972); *Modernist Painting and Sculpture: Hofmann, Motherwell, Noland, Stella, Caro, Murray, Steiner* (1972).

9. Commercial galleries were also important to development of the community in Edmonton, for example: Martin Gerard, Woltjen/Udell, Hett Gallery, Latitude 53, Ringhouse Gallery, and the defunct Sub-Gallery all served as focal points for those artists not intent on modernism.

10. These purchases include works by late modernists such as Kenneth Noland, Walter Darby Bannard, Stanley Boxer, Darryl Hughto, Jules Olitski, Larry Poons, Susan Roth, Michael Steiner, and Sidney Tillim.

11. Clement Greenberg, "Towards a Newer Laocoon," in Francis Frascina, *Pollack and After: The Critical Debate* (New York: Harper & Row 1985), p.43.

12. Not all artists in Edmonton wished to participate in this international, modernist discourse. Issues of regionalist/nationalist art versus international modernism created a polarized visual arts community. These issues are elaborated upon in Terry Fenton and Karen Wilkin, *Modern Painting in Canada* (Edmonton: Hurtig Publishers Ltd., 1978).

13. Commercial spaces such as Canadian Art Galleries, Paul Kuhn Fine Arts, Virginia Christopher, and more recently, Stride, are important forums where, through exhibition opportunities and promotion, artists gain regional as well as national recognition.

14. Nancy Tousley, "Couples' Work Reflects Creative Dialogue," *Calgary Herald*, November 3, 1983.

15. Leslie Dawn, "William MacDonnell," *Vanguard* (February/March 1986), pp. 41-42.

16. John Bentley Mays, "Three Artists from Calgary," *Globe and Mail*, Toronto, June 13, 1985.

17. Nancy Tousley, "Synthesis of Experiences Embraced," *Calgary Herald*, March 14, 1986.

18. Jessica Bradley and Diana Nemiroff, *Songs of Experience* (Ottawa: National Gallery of Canada, 1986).

19. Greg Bellerby, *Jeffrey Spalding: Recent Paintings*, (Victoria, B.C. Art Gallery of Greater Victoria, December 13, 1984 - February 3, 1985).

20. Peter White, "Don't Forget: Keep Your Head Down" introduction to *Billy J. McCarroll, How To Play A Winning Game Your Natural Way: The Metaphor Continues* (Regina, SK: Dunlop Art Gallery)

NOTES

A lberta Government. "The Banff Centre's 50th." *Visual Arts Newsletter*, 5(3) (Summer 1983). Edmonton: Alberta Culture.

A lberta Government. "The Coste House 1946-59." *Visual Arts Newsletter*, 7(4) (Issue 30, August 1985) Edmonton: Alberta Culture.

A lberta Government. "The Coste House 1946-59." *Visual Arts Newsletter*, 7(5) (Issue 31, October 1985) Edmonton: Alberta Culture.

A lberta Government. "The Coste House 1946-59." *Visual Arts Newsletter*, 7(6) (Issue 32, December 1985) Edmonton: Alberta Culture.

B ates, Maxwell. "Some Problems of Environment." *Highlights*, 2(8) (December 1948) (Alberta Society of Artists).

B ates, Maxwell. "Art and Snobbery." *Highlights*, 1(1) (March 1949) (Alberta Society of Artists).

B ates, Maxwell. "The Flight from Meaning in Painting." *Canadian Art*, 11(2) (Winter 1954).

B ates, Maxwell. "Some Reflections on Art in Alberta." *Canadian Art*, 12(1) (Autumn 1955).

B ates, Maxwell. "Divided We Fall." *Highlights* (Summer 1957) (Alberta Society of Artists).

B attock, Gregory. (Ed.). *Minimal Art: A Critical Anthology*. New York: E.P. Dutton & Co., 1968.

B ellerby, Greg. *Jeffrey Spalding: Recent Paintings*. Victoria, B.C.: Art Gallery of Greater Victoria.

B entley Mays, John. "Three artists from Calgary at the Wynick/Tuck Gallery." *Globe and Mail*, Toronto, June 13, 1985.

B ingham, Russell. *The Big Picture: Large-Scale Landscape Painting on the Prairies*. Edmonton: The Edmonton Art Gallery, 1981.

B ingham, Russell. "Variety with a Focus." *Update*, 6(4) (July/August 1984) (Edmonton Art Gallery).

B ingham, Russell. "Abstract Painting in Edmonton." *Update*, 7(4) (September/October 1986) (Edmonton Art Gallery).

B loore, Ronald L. "The Prairies: To Assert Man's Presence." *Artscanada*, 26(6) (December 1969)

B radley, Jessica and Diana Nemiroff. *Songs of Experience*. Ottawa: National Gallery of Canada, 1986.

B ringhurst, Robert, Geoffrey James, Russell Keziere, and Doris Shadbolt. *Visions: Contemporary Art in Canada*. Vancouver: Douglas & McIntyre, 1983.

B uchanan, Donald W. "Prairie Metamorphosis." *Canadian Art*, 11(1) (Autumn 1953).

B uchanan, Donald W. "A Prairie Approach to a Canadian Vision." *Canadian Art*, 20(1) (January/February 1963).

B uchloh, Benjamin H.D., Serge Guilbaut, and David Solkin (Eds.). *Modernism and Modernity: The Vancouver Conference Papers*. Halifax, NS: The Press of the Nova Scotia College of Art and Design, 1983.

B urnett, David, and Marilyn Schiff. *Contemporary Canadian Painting*. Edmonton: Hurtig Publishers Ltd., 1983.

C ollinson, Helen. *H.G. Glyde in Canada*. Edmonton: The Edmonton Art Gallery, 1974.

D avidson, J.H. " Alberta Art Foundation: Filling a Gap." *Update*, 6(4) (July/August 1985) (Edmonton Art Gallery).

D awn, Leslie. "William MacDonnell." *Vanguard*, (February/March 1986).

D illow, Nancy. "Emma Lake Workshops 1955-1973." Regina SK: Norman MacKenzie Art Gallery, 1973. (newsletter)

F enton, Terry. "Olitski and Saskatchewan." Regina, SK: Norman MacKenzie Art Gallery, April 1970. (newsletter)

F enton, Terry. "High Culture in Prairie Canada." *ARTnews*, 73(7) (September 1974).

F enton, Terry. "Abstraction West: Emma Lake and After." *The National Gallery of Canada Journal*, No. 11, March 1, 1976.

F enton, Terry. "The Canada Council 25th Anniversary Show: With an Aside About New Edmonton Art." *Update*, 3(3) (May/June 1982) (Edmonton Art Gallery).

F enton, Terry, and Karen Wilkin. *Modern Painting in Canada* Edmonton: Hurtig Publishers Ltd., 1978.

F leming, Carolyn. "Autonomy." *Visual Arts Newsletter*, 6(4) (Issue 24, August 1984). Edmonton: Alberta Culture.

F orbes, J. Allison, *J.B. Taylor*. Edmonton: The Edmonton Art Gallery and University of Alberta, Department of Art and Design, 1973.

BIBLIOGRAPHY

F oster, Hal (Ed.). *The Anti-Aesthetic: Essays on Postmodern Culture*. Port Townsend, WA: Bay Press, 1983.

F oster, Hal. *Recodings: Art, Spectacle, Cultural Politics*. Port Townsend, Wa: Bay Press, 1985.

F rascara, Jorge (Ed). Staff Exhibition, *Department of Art and Design, University of Alberta*. Edmonton: Department of Art and Design, University of Alberta, 1985.

F rascina, Francis (Ed) *Pollock and After: The Critical Debate*. New York: Harper & Row, 1985.

G reenberg, Clement. "Clement Greenberg's View of Art on the Prairies: Painting and Sculpture in Prairie Canada Today." *Canadian Art*, 20(2) (March/April 1963).

G reenberg, Clement. "Post-painterly Abstraction." *Art International*, 8 (Summer 1964).

G reenfield, Val. *New Image Alberta*. Calgary: Lavalin Inc., 1982.

G reenfield, Val. "Introduction." *A Measure of Success: Graduates of the Alberta College of Art 1963-1984*. Calgary: Alberta College of Art, 1985.

G reenfield, Val. *Founders of the Alberta College of Art*. Calgary: Alberta College of Art, 1986.

G ribbon, Michael J. *Walter J. Phillips*. Ottawa: National Gallery of Canada, National Museums of Canada, 1978.

G uernsey, Terry. *Maxwell Bates in Retrospect 1921-1971*. Vancouver, BC: Vancouver Art Gallery, 1973.

H ardy, W.G. (Editor-in-Chief). *Alberta Golden Jubilee Anthology*. Toronto: McClelland & Stewart Ltd., 1955.

H arper, J. Russell. *Painting in Canada: A History*. Toronto: University of Toronto Press, 1966.

H arper, J. Russell. *Paul Kane 1810-1871*. Fort Worth, TX: Amon Carter Museum of Western Art; Ottawa: National Gallery of Canada, 1971.

H arper, J. Russell. *William G.R. Hind 1833-1889*. Ottawa: National Gallery of Canada, 1976.

H arris, Lawren. "An Essay on Abstract Painting." *Canadian Art* 6(3) (Spring 1949)

H eath, Terrence. *Western Untitled*. Calgary: Glenbow Museum, 1976.

H eiman, Trudie (Ed.). *Latitude 53: A Decade*. Edmonton: Latitude 53, 1983.

H ubbard, R.H. "A Climate for the Arts." *Canadian Art*, 12(4) (Summer 1955)

H ubbard, R.H., and J.R. Ostiguy. *Three Hundred Years of Canadian Art*. Ottawa: National Gallery of Canada, 1967

J ackson, A.Y. "Banff School of Fine Arts." *Canadian Art*, 3(4) (July 1946).

K err, Illingworth H. *Fifty Years a Painter*. Calgary: Alberta College of Art, 1973.

K ey, A.F. "The Calgary Art Centre." *Canadian Art*, 4(3) (May 1947).

K ing, John. "A Documented Study of the Artists' Workshop at Emma Lake, Saskatchewan of the School of Art, University of Saskatchewan, Regina, from 1955 to 1970." B.F.A. thesis, University of Manitoba, 1970.

K rauss, Rosalind E. *The Originality of the Avant-Garde and Other Modernist Myths*. Cambridge, MA: MIT Press, 1985.

K uspit, Donald B. *Clement Greenberg: Art Critic*. Madison WI: University of Wisconsin Press, 1979.

L ord, Barry. *The History of Painting in Canada: Towards a People's Art*. Toronto: NC Press, 1974.

M abie, Don (Ed.). *The First Ten: 1975-1985*. Calgary: Off Centre Centre, 1985.

M ays, John Bentley. "Three Artists from Calgary." *Globe and Mail*, June 13, 1985.

M cGregor, Gaile. *The Wacousta Syndrome: Explorations in the Canadian Landscape*. Toronto: University of Toronto Press, 1985.

M cGregor, J.G. *Edmonton: A History*. Edmonton: Hurtig Publishers, 1967.

M cKay, Arthur. "Emma Lake Artists' Workshop: An Appreciation." *Canadian Art*, 21(5) (September/October 1964).

M ellen, Peter. *The Group of Seven*. Toronto: McClelland & Stewart, 1970.

N asgaard, Roald, *The Mystic North: Symbolist Landscape Painting in Northern Europe and North America 1890-1940*. Toronto: Art Gallery of Ontario, 1984.

N icoll, J. McL. "Alberta Hangs Up Its Chaps." Introduction to *Jubilee Exhibition of Alberta Paintings*. Calgary: Calgary Allied Arts Centre, 1955 (Coste House).

O uellet, Raymond. *W.L. Stevenson*. Edmonton: The Edmonton Art Gallery, Extension Department, 1976.

O uellet, Raymond. *Seven Prairie Painters*. Toronto: Art Gallery of Ontario, 1978.

P incus-Witten, Robert. *Postminimalism: American Art of the Decade*. New York: Oolp Press, 1981

P ollock, Ann. *Jock Macdonald: Retrospective Exhibition*. Ottawa: National Gallery of Canada, 1969.

R ender, Lorne E. *A.C. Leighton: Art Series No. 3*. Calgary: Glenbow-Alberta Institute, 1971.

R ender, Lorne E. *The Mountains and The Sky*. Calgary: Glenbow-Alberta Institute and McClelland & Stewart West Ltd., 1974

S ilcox, David. "Canadian Art in the Sixties." *Canadian Art*, 23(1) (January 1966).

S immins, Richard B. *Five Painters from Regina*. Ottawa: National Gallery of Canada, 1961.

S tocking, John R. "Promotional Art History and the Iconography of Style." *Parachute*, 16 (Autumn 1979).

T hompson, David. "A Canadian Scene." *Studio International*, 176(90) (October 1968)

T ousley, Nancy. "The Calgary Art Scene." *Update*, (September/October 1980) (Edmonton Art Gallery).

T ousley, Nancy. "Couples' Work Reflects Creative Dialogue." *Calgary Herald*, November 3, 1983.

T ousley, Nancy. *Seven Artists from Alberta: Art in This Region*. London: Canada House Cultural Centre Gallery and Edmonton, AB: Alberta Culture, 1984.

T ousley, Nancy. "Calgary Artists Show Well in Toronto." *Visual Arts Newsletter*, 7(6) (Issue 32, December 1985). Edmonton: Alberta Culture.

T ousley, Nancy. "Synthesis of Experiences Embraced." *Calgary Herald*, March 14, 1986.

T ousley, Nancy. "Roots, Rejections and Rewards in Calgary." *Canadian Art* 3(16) (Fall 1986).

T ownsend, William. "Notes: By Way of Introduction and Dedication." Introduction to *Canadian Art Today*. London: Studio International, 1970.

V arley, Christopher. "Art, Science and the Canadian Character." *Update*, 4(2) (March/April, 1983) (Edmonton Art Gallery)

V arley, Christopher. *Winnipeg West: Painting and Sculpture in Western Canada 1945-1970*. Edmonton: The Edmonton Art Gallery, 1983.

V entures, Duck. *Marion Nicoll: A Retrospective, 1959-1971*. Edmonton: The Edmonton Art Gallery, 1975.

W allis, Brian. *Art After Modernism: Rethinking Representation*. New York/Boston: New Museum of Contemporary Art, NY; David R. Godine, Publisher, 1984.

W hite, Peter. *Billy J. McCarroll: How to Play a Winning Game Your Natural Way: The Metaphor Continues*. Regina SK: Dunlop Art Gallery.

W ilkin, Karen. "Canada: A Report From The West." *Art in America*, 3 (May/June 1972).

W ilkin, Karen. *Art in Alberta: Paul Kane to the Present*. Edmonton: The Edmonton Art Gallery, 1973.

W ilkin, Karen. *The Group of Seven in the Rockies*. Edmonton and Banff, AB: The Edmonton Art Gallery and the Peter Whyte Gallery, 1974.

W ilkin, Karen. "Rugged Individualists with No Urge to Roam. " *ARTnews*, 78(2) (February 1979).

W illiamson, Moncrieff. *Through Canadian Eyes: Trends and Influences in Canadian Art 1815-1965*. Calgary: Glenbow-Alberta Institute, 1976.

W ithrow, William. *Contemporary Canadian Painting*. Toronto: McClelland & Stewart Ltd, 1972.

W ylie, Liz. "The Underside of Edmonton." *Vanguard*, 13(4) (May 1984).

GIUSEPPE G. ALBI

BORN:
1946, Italy

EDUCATION:
1966-68
Alberta College of Art, Calgary

1968-69
L'Ecole des Beaux Arts, Montreal

SELECTED EXHIBITIONS:
Group
1981
Recent acquisitions, Alberta Art Foundation, Edmonton

1983
*Latitude 53 Society of Artists
10th Anniversary Exhibition,*
Latitude 53, Edmonton

1985
Studio Watch, The Edmonton Art Gallery

Abstract Painting in Edmonton
The Edmonton Art Gallery

Giuseppe Albi exhibits regularly at the Woltjen/Udell Gallery, Edmonton.

SELECTED BIBLIOGRAPHY:
Bingham, Russell. "Giuseppe Albi: Recent Paintings." *Update,* (8)1 (January/February 1987) (Edmonton Art Gallery)

Chalmers, Ron. "Abstract Painting in Edmonton." *Edmonton Journal,* September 13, 1986

Walker, Mike. "High Tech, High Profile." *Visual Arts Newsletter,* 8(46) (August 1986)

Heiman, Trudie. "Abstract Painting in Edmonton." *Update,* 7(4) (January/February 1986) (Edmonton Art Gallery)

————. *Latitude 53: A Decade.* Edmonton, AB: Latitude 53, 1983

Adams, James. "Artist finally came home to make his own statement." *Edmonton Journal,* January 3, 1981

JACK ANDERSON

BORN:
1949, Lethbridge

EDUCATION:
1976
BFA, University of Calgary

1979
MFA, University of Cincinnati, Ohio

SELECTED EXHIBITIONS:
Group
1980
Rockwell Kent Gallery, State University of New York (S.U.N.Y.) at Plattsburgh

Miami International Print Biennial, Metropolitan Museum, Miami, Florida

Columbus Cultural Center Gallery, Columbus, Ohio

Wittenburg University, Springfield, Ohio

City of Middleton City Centre, Middleton, Ohio

French Art Colony, Gallipolis, Ohio

1982
S.E.T., Nickle Museum, Calgary
*8 Frames: Translations from the Sanscrit
(a Film),* Off Centre Centre Art Gallery, Calgary

1983
Nickle Arts Museum, Calgary

1984
Currents, Off Centre Centre, Calgary

Graphex 9, Art Gallery of Brant, Brantford, Ontario (National print and drawing exhibition)

1985
Nickle Arts Museum, Calgary
(*ICON I* with John Will)

10th Anniversary Show, Off Centre Centre, Calgary (*ICON 11* with John Will)

Beaver House Gallery, Edmonton

ICON III, (with John Will)
Kamloops Public Art Gallery, Kamloops, B.C.

Whirly-Gig, Alberta College of Art, Calgary (*ICON IV* with John Will)

Video Culture International, Toronto

The Jewels in the Crowns, Skyroom, Calgary (Performance with John Will)

1986
Nickle Arts Museum, Calgary
(*ICON V* with John Will)

Anxiously Awaiting Midnight, Southern Alberta Art Gallery, Lethbridge

Painted Bride Gallery, Philadelphia, Penn.

Shrimp Boars, Izobizo, Calgary
(Performance with John Will)

SELECTED BIBLIOGRAPHY:
Laviolette, Mary-Beth. *Anxiously Awaiting Midnight.* Lethbridge, AB: Southern Alberta Art Gallery, 1986.

Tousley, Nancy. "Roots, Rejections and Rewards in Calgary." *Canadian Art,* 3(16) (Fall 1986)

Varga, Vincent. "Jack Anderson." *Vanguard,* 15(2) (April/May 1986) pp. 44-45

Anonymous. "Triple Bill Opens SAAG." *Lethbridge Herald,* February 1, 1986

Laviolette, Mary-Beth. "Currents." *Vanguard,* 13(4) (May 1984) p. 39

Tousley, Nancy. "Artists Turn On Power in Currents." *Calgary Herald,* February 19, 1984

————. "Life without electricity interesting." *Calgary Herald,* February 19, 1984

Allen, Karyn, (Ed.). *S.E.T.: an installation.* Calgary, AB: Nickle Arts Musuem, 1982

Tousley, Nancy. "Magic Installation explores artist's India experience." *Calgary Herald,* June 12, 1982

————. "Anderson Exhibition Shows Value of Installation Art." *Calgary Herald,* May 15, 1982

Jack Anderson is now teaching at the Nova Scotia School of Art and Design.

64

JOHN G. J. BROCKE

BORN:
1953, Edmonton

EDUCATION:
1981
Graduated from the Alberta College of Art, Calgary

SELECTED EXHIBITIONS:
Group
1980
Artists under Construction,
Muttart Gallery, Calgary

1984
New Alberta Artists, Muttart Gallery, Calgary

Six Calgary Realists, touring exhibition organized by Alberta Culture

Beaver House Gallery, Edmonton

Petro-Canada Art Gallery, Calgary

1985
Grande Prairie Art Gallery, Grande Prairie

Three Artists from Calgary, Wynick/Tuck Gallery, Toronto

Still Wet, Glenbow Museum, Calgary

Solo
1984
Gulf Canada Square Gallery, Calgary

SELECTED BIBLIOGRAPHY:
Tousley, Nancy. "Artist keeps faith with Realism." *Calgary Herald,* March 30, 1986

————. "Painter celebrates images of reality." *Calgary Herald,* June 30, 1985

CHRIS CRAN

BORN:
1949, Ocean Falls, British Columbia

EDUCATION:
1975-76
Kootenay School of Art, Nelson, B.C.

1976-79
Alberta College of Art, Calgary

SELECTED EXHIBITIONS:
Group
1980
Mostly Smaller Works, Off Centre Centre, Calgary

Some Drawings by Some Albertans,
Alberta College of Art Gallery, Calgary

1985
A Measure of Success: Graduates of the Alberta College of Art, 1974 - 1984, Alberta College of Art Gallery, Calgary

5 Plus 5, Off Centre Centre, Calgary

Solo
1980
MIU Student Gallery, Fairfield, Iowa

1986
Stride Gallery, Calgary

SELECTED BIBLIOGRAPHY:
Tousley, Nancy. "Local Artists Look To Themselves in Amusing Show." *Calgary Herald,* September 26, 1986

————. "Roots, Rejections and Rewards in Calgary." *Canadian Art,* 3(16) (September 1986) pp.72-79

————. "5 Plus 5 Worth a Stop on Sunday's Art Walk." *Calgary Herald,* September 27, 1985

EVA DIENER

BORN:
1939, Kusnacht, Switzerland

EDUCATION:
BA, BSc, Zurich, Switzerland

Zurich Kunstgewerbeschule, Switzerland

Melbourne Technical School, Australia

SELECTED EXHIBITIONS:
Group
1980
GSMBK, Kunsthaus, Zurich

Alberta Drawing, Alberta College of Art Gallery, Calgary

1981
Kunstzene, Zurich

1982
Kunstgewerbemuseum, Zurich

1984
Contemporary Women Artists,
Zurich, Basel, Bern, Olten

Rastorfer Gallery, Munich, West Germany

City of Zurich

1985
GSMBK Kunsthaus, Zurich

1986
GSMBK Helmhaus, Zurich

Solo
1980
The Edmonton Art Gallery

Hufschmid Gallery

1982
Walcheturm Gallery, Zurich

1984
Vanderleelie Gallery, Edmonton

1985
Walcheturm Gallery, Zurich

1986
Kunstmuseum Kanton Thurgau, Kartause Ittingen, Switzerland

1987
Brugg City Art Gallery, Switzerland

ALAN DUNNING

BORN:
1950, Teddington, Middlesex, U.K.

EDUCATION:
1968-69
Chester College of Art, Chester, Cheshire, U.K., Foundation

1969-72
Bath Academy of Art, Corsham, Wiltshire, U.K., Diploma A.D. Painting

1975-77
University of Alberta, Edmonton, MVA Printmaking, Incomplete

SELECTED EXHIBITIONS:
Group
1980
Monuments, Off Centre Centre, Calgary

1981
Some Drawings by Some Albertans, Alberta College of Art Gallery, Calgary

Prints from the Files, Player Press, Chicago, Illinois

Miniatures, Latitude 53, Edmonton

Triangle. Public Installation/Performance, Edmonton

1982
Player Press, Chicago, Illinois, Graphics

Miniatures, Latitude 53, Edmonton

Exceptional Pass, Peter Whyte Gallery, Banff, Alberta

12 Red Squares Distributed Across Europe (With William MacDonnell)

Red Square (With Emrys Morgan), Todmorden, Yorks, U.K.

1984
In Triplicate (Dunning, May, Senini), Latitude 53, Edmonton

Graphex 9, Art Gallery of Brant, Brantford, Ontario,

1985
Still Wet, Glenbow Museum, Calgary,

The Myth of Exceptional Pass, Peter White Gallery, Banff, Alberta,

Ten Years After, Off Centre Centre, Calgary; Beaver House, Edmonton

1986
Scale, Alberta College of Art Gallery, Calgary

Eighth Annual Dalhousie Drawing Show, Dalhousie University, Halifax

Solo
1981
621 Triangles Distributed ..., Latitude 53, Edmonton

1983
Not exactly as illustrated, Off Centre Centre, Calgary

1987
Soup, Stride Gallery, Calgary

SELECTED BIBLIOGRAPHY:
Tousley, Nancy. "Artist weaves imagery in gallery installation." *Calgary Herald,* March 19, 1987

Greenfield, Valerie (Ed.). *Scale.* Calgary: Alberta College of Art Gallery, 1986

Butler, Sheila. *Eighth Annual Dalhousie Drawing Show.* Halifax, NS: Dalhousie University, 1986

Varga, Vincent. *Still Wet.* Calgary, AB: Glenbow Museum, 1985

Brown, Elizabeth. *The Myth of the Exceptional Pass.* Banff, AB: Peter Whyte Gallery, 1985

Mabie, Don (Ed.). *Ten Years After.* Calgary, AB: Off Centre Centre, 1985

Brown, Elizabeth. *Exceptional Pass.* Banff, AB: Peter Whyte Gallery, 1982

Mabie, Don. *Some Drawings by Some Albertans.* Calgary, AB: Alberta College of Art Gallery, 1981

Alan Dunning teaches painting at the Alberta College of Art, Calgary

WAYNE GILES

BORN:
1947, Calgary

EDUCATION:
1973
BA, University of Calgary

1977
BFA, University of Calgary

SELECTED EXHIBITIONS:
Group
1981
Construction Work, Off Centre Centre, Calgary

1982
Contemporary Work From Calgary, Gallery Quan, Toronto

New Image Alberta, national touring exhibition organized by the Alberta College of Art

Western Images, James Ulrich Gallery, Calgary

Small Works, James Ulrich Gallery, Calgary

1983
Wayne Giles/Laura Pope, James Ulrich Gallery

Studio Sculpture, Latitude 53, Edmonton

1984
New Acquisitions, Alberta Art Foundation, Beaver House Gallery, Edmonton

1985
Burns Visual Arts Society, Open Studio, Calgary

Burns Visual Arts Society At Off Centre Centre, Off Centre Centre, Calgary

The First Ten, Off Centre Centre, Calgary; Beaver House, Edmonton

1986
Exhibition of Calgary Artists, organized by Paul Kuhn Fine Art at Nova Ltd.

Burns Visual Arts Society, Open Studio, Calgary

Solo
1985
American Beauties, Paul Kuhn Gallery, Calgary

SELECTED BIBLIOGRAPHY:
Tousley, Nancy. "Giles Gives Witty Analysis." *Calgary Herald,* April 19, 1985

JOHN HALL

BORN:
1943, Edmonton

EDUCATION:
1960-65
Alberta College of Art, Calgary

1965-66
Instituto de Allende, Mexico

SELECTED EXHIBITIONS:
Group
1980
Painting in Alberta: An Historical Survey,
The Edmonton Art Gallery

R.C.A. Alberta, The Nickle Arts Museum,
University of Calgary

The Rose Museum Sells Out, Off Centre Centre,
Calgary

Mostly Smaller Works, Off Centre Centre, Calgary

1981
Art Bank Exhibition, Acadia University Art Gallery,
Wolfville, Nova Scotia

Realism: Structure and Illusion, touring exhibition
organized by The Macdonald Stewart Art Centre,
Guelph, Ontario

1982
The Winnipeg Perspective - Post-Pop Realism,
Winnipeg Art Gallery

1983
Prepaid Miniature Art Sale, London Regional Art
Gallery, London, Ontario

1983-84
*The Hand Holding The Brush, Self Portraits by
Canadian Artists 1825-1983,* touring exhibition
organized by the London Regional Art Gallery,
London, Ontario

1984
Seven Artists from Alberta: Art in This Region,
International touring exhibition: Canada House,
London, England; Canadian Cultural Centre,
Brussels, Belgium; Canadian Culture Centre,
Paris, France

Now Showing in Europe, Beaver House Gallery,
Edmonton

1985
The First Ten, Off Centre Centre, Calgary

5 Plus 5, Off Centre Centre, Calgary

*A Measure of Success: Graduates of the Alberta
College of Art 1963-1973,* Alberta College of Art
Gallery, Calgary

La Boite dans L'Art, Centre d'Exposition,
Aylmer, Quebec

Solo
1980
*John Hall: Paintings and Auxiliary Works
1969-1978,* touring exhibition

John Hall Paintings/Maquettes, P.S. 1, New York;
Off Centre Centre, Calgary

The Mendel Art Gallery, Saskatoon

1982
The Southern Alberta Art Gallery,
Lethbridge

The Edmonton Art Gallery

1985
Off Centre Centre, Calgary

John Hall regularly exhibits at the Wynick/Tuck
Gallery, Toronto.

SELECTED BIBLIOGRAPHY:
Mays, John Bentley. "Hall's Comfortable as Odd
Man Out." *Globe and Mail,* May 18, 1985

Burnett, David. "John Hall: New Paintings."
Canadian Art, 2(3) (Fall/September 1985) p. 89

Greenfield, Valerie. *A Measure of Success.*
Calgary, AB: Alberta College of Art Gallery, 1985

Mabie, Don. *The First Ten: 1975-1985.*
Calgary, AB: Off Centre Centre, 1985

Tousley, Nancy. *Seven Artists from Alberta: Art in
this Region.* London, England: Canada House
Cultural Centre Gallery and Edmonton, AB:
Alberta Culture, 1984

————. "Alberta Goes to Europe." excerpt
from *Seven Artists in Alberta: Art in this Region.*
Visual Arts Newsletter, 7(3) (June 1984)

Varley, Christopher. "Tourist Series and Toy
Series." *Update,* 4(1) (January/February 1983)
(Edmonton Art Gallery)

Burnett, David and Marilyn Schiff. *Contemporary
Canadian Art.* Edmonton, AB:
Hurtig Publishers Ltd., 1983

Stacey, Robert. *The Hand Holding the Brush: Self
Portraits by Canadian Artists.* London, ONT:
The London Regional Art Gallery, 1983

Mays, John Bentley. "The Snakes in the Garden."
Essay in *Visions: Contemporary Art in Canada.*
Robert Bringhurst; Geoffrey James; Russell
Keziere; Doris Shadbolt (Ed.), Vancouver, BC:
Douglas and McIntyre Ltd., 1983

Anonymous. "John Hall Interview." *Visual Arts
Newsletter,* 4(1) (Winter 1982)

Madill, Shirley. *Post-Pop Realism: The Winnipeg
Perspective 1982.* Winnipeg, MAN:
The Winnipeg Art Gallery, 1982

Tousley, Nancy. *John Hall: Tourists and Toys.*
Toronto, ONT: Wynick/Tuck Gallery and
Lethbridge, AB: Southern Alberta Art Gallery,
1982

————. "Artist's work linked to frontier
tradition of the tall tale." *Calgary Herald,*
February 26, 1981

Mays, John Bentley. "Calgary Artist finds
inspiration in mass-produced miscellany."
Globe and Mail, April 13, 1981

Besant, Derek Michael. "John Hall - The Artist as
Tourist." *Artmagazine,* 13(55)
(September/October 1981) p. 46

Devonshire Baker, Suzanne. *Artists of Alberta.*
Edmonton, AB: University of Alberta Press, 1980

Lipman, Marci and Louise Lipman. *Images:
Contemporary Canadian Realism.* Toronto, ONT:
Lester and Orpen Dennys, 1980

Burnett, David. "John Hall." *Artscanada.*
(234/235) (April/May 1980) p. 40

Fry, Philip. "John Hall: Paintings and Auxiliary
Works, 1969-1978." *Parachute,* 18
(Spring 1980) pp. 9-11

Hammond, Lois. "Extraordinary Images from an
Ordinary Man." *Western Living,* March, 1980

John Hall teaches at the University of Calgary.

JOICE M. HALL

BORN:
1943, Edmonton

EDUCATION:
1961-65
Alberta College of Art, Calgary

1976
C.C. Travel grant to New York
Travelled to Europe in the fall

SELECTED EXHIBITIONS:
Group
1980
Some Drawings by Some Albertans,
Alberta College of Art Gallery, Calgary

1981
New Acquisitions, Glenbow Museum,
Calgary

Body Parts, SUB Gallery, Edmonton

1982
Canada Council Art Bank Exhibition,
I.G.A. Gallery, Toronto

1983
Le Nu et L'erotisme Dans L'Art Contemporain,
University of Quebec, Montreal

Choices, Provincial Museum, Edmonton

1984
Edge and Image, Concordia, Montreal

Ten Years After, Off Centre Centre,
Calgary; Beaver House Gallery, Edmonton

1985
*A Measure of Success: Graduates of the Alberta
College of Art 1963-1973,* Alberta College of
Art Gallery, Calgary

Solo
1981
New Work, Off Centre Centre, Calgary

1982
Joice M. Hall/Paintings, Drawings, Gallery Quan,
Toronto

1984
Banff Landscapes, Paul Kuhn Fine Arts Gallery,
Calgary

1986
Spaces and Places, The Nickle Arts Museum,
Calgary; organized by the Alberta Art Foundation

1987
Figures, Paul Kuhn Fine Arts, Calgary

Floating, Southern Alberta Art Gallery,
Lethbridge

SELECTED BIBLIOGRAPHY:
Tousley, Nancy. "Artist Captures Scope, Grandeur
of the Rockies." *Calgary Herald,* June 1, 1986

Anonymous. "Local Artists Look to Selves in
Amusing Show. " *Calgary Herald,*
September 26, 1986

Anonymous. "Alberta Artists at the Leighton
Artist Colony." *Visual Arts Newsletter,*
7 (June 1985) p. 10

Tousley, Nancy. "Artist Experiments."
Calgary Herald, February 1, 1985

Matousek, Phylis. "Businessman Sees Art As An
Industry." *Edmonton Journal,* February 27, 1983.

Tousley, Nancy. "Painter Thumbs Her Nose at
Taboo." *Calgary Herald,* September 10, 1981

DOUGLAS HAYNES

BORN:
1936, Regina

EDUCATION:
1958
Graduated from the Provincial Institute of
Technology and Art (now Alberta College of Art)

1960-61
Studied at the Royal Academy of Art,
The Hague, Netherlands

SELECTED EXHIBITIONS:
1980
Alberta Now, The Edmonton Art Gallery

1981
Heritage of Jack Bush, McIntosh Gallery,
Oshawa, Ontario

1982
Threshold of Colour, The Edmonton Art Gallery

1983
*Winnipeg West: Painting and Sculpture in
Western Canada, 1945 - 1970,* The Edmonton
Art Gallery

1985
Abstractions X 4, Canada House, London,
England; Bonn, West Germany; Paris, France

1986
Abstract Painting in Edmonton,
The Edmonton Art Gallery

Founders exhibition, Alberta College of Art,
Calgary

Solo
1980
Southern Alberta Art Gallery, Lethbridge

1981
Mendel Art Centre, Saskatoon

1983
Norman MacKenzie Art Gallery, Regina

1985
*Cubism Revisited: Douglas Haynes, a five year
survey,* The Edmonton Art Gallery

SELECTED BIBLIOGRAPHY:
Bingham, Russell. "Cubism Revisited." *Update*, 6(1) (January/February 1985) pp. 8-9 (Edmonton Art Gallery)

Varley, Christopher. *Winnipeg West: Painting and Sculpture in Western Canada, 1945-1970*. Edmonton: The Edmonton Art Gallery, 1983

Anonymous. "Mandarin's Jacket." *ARTnews*, 82(94) (January 1983)

Tousley, Nancy. "Visual Arts." *Calgary Herald*, May 1, 1981

Cochran, Bente. "The Visual Arts in Edmonton: An International Focus." *Artswest*, 6(5) (May 1981) pp. 14-19

GERALD HUSHLAK

BORN:
1944, Andrew, Alberta

EDUCATION:
1973
Post graduate degree from Royal College of Art, London, England - M.A.R.C.A.

Undergraduate study at University of Alberta, Edmonton, University of Calgary, and University of California, Berkeley.

SELECTED EXHIBITIONS:
Electra Exhibition, Museum of Modern Art, Paris, France

SELECTED BIBLIOGRAPHY:
Van Hersel, Eric. "From the Mail." *Last Issue*, (May/June 1984) p. 4

Elton, Heather. "Whirl." *Last Issue*, (May/June 1984) pp. 9-10

Mustak, Alan. "Some Like it Hot: Hushlack Back in the Feminist's Doghouse." *Alberta Report*, March 5, 1984

Sheppard, J. "House That Gerald Built." *Alberta Report*, May 24, 1982

Stocking, John. "New Computer Art." *Art Magazine*, 12(52) (February/March 1981) pp. 31-35

Richards, Jean. "Hushlak Communicates With Color." *Edmonton Journal*, April 17, 1980

Keziere, Russell. "Gerald Hushlak." *Vanguard*, 9(1) (February 1980) p. 32

Gerald Hushlak teaches at the University of Calgary.

TERRENCE KELLER

BORN:
1947, Edmonton

EDUCATION:
1969-73
Alberta College of Art, Calgary

1973
Michael Steiner Workshop, The Edmonton Art Gallery

1982
Triangle Workshop, Pine Plains, N.Y.

SELECTED EXHIBITIONS:
Group
1980
Alberta Now, The Edmonton Art Gallery

1981
Alberta Contemporary Art, Glenbow Museum, Calgary

Keller, Sutton, Saito, The Edmonton Art Gallery

Modernist Painting and Sculpture, Glenbow Museum, Calgary

1982
Triangle Workshop Exhibition, Pine Plains, New York

1983
My Favorite Picture, The Edmonton Art Gallery

1984
Keller, Christie, Perehudoff, Plear, The Gallery, Saskatoon

1985
A Measure of Success: Graduates of the Alberta College of Art 1963-1973, Alberta College of Art Gallery, Calgary

1986
Abstract Painting In Edmonton, The Edmonton Art Gallery

International Contemporary Art Fair, Los Angeles, California

Solo
1985
Triangle Center, New York, N.Y.

Terrence Keller exhibits regularly at the Martin Gerard Gallery and Woltjen/Udell Gallery, Edmonton.

SELECTED BIBLIOGRAPHY:
Fenton, Terry. "A Year in Review: 'Canadians'."
Update, 4(2) (March/April 1983) p. 10
(Edmonton Art Gallery)

————. "Surprises, 1981: The Art Year
in Review." *Update*, 3(1) (January/February 1982)
p. 12 (Edmonton Art Gallery)

Cochran, Bente. "The Visual Arts in Edmonton: An
International Focus." *Artswest*, 6(5)
(May 1981) pp. 14-19

DON D. KOTTMANN

BORN:
1946, St. Louis, Missouri

EDUCATION:
1964-68
BFA, University of Kansas, Lawrence, Kansas

1968-70
MFA, University of Washington, Seattle

SELECTED EXHIBITIONS:
Group
1984
Now Showing In Europe, Beaver House Gallery,
Edmonton

Seven Artists From Alberta: Art in this Region,
International touring exhibition: Canada House,
London, England: Canada Cultural Centre,
Brussels, Belgium: Canadian Culture Centre,
Paris, France

1986
UNESCO 40th Anniversary Travelling Exhibition,
organized by the United Nations Education,
Scientific and Cultural Organization

Self Image, Off Centre Centre, Calgary

Solo
1983
New Paintings, Off Centre Centre, Calgary

SELECTED BIBLIOGRAPHY:
Tousley, Nancy. "Gallery Serves Up Pot-Pourri."
Calgary Herald, August 8, 1986

————. "Artist Relates Work to Life Experiences."
Calgary Herald, July 27, 1986

————. "Local Painter Makes Bid for
Mainstream" *Calgary Herald,*
June 14, 1985

————. *Seven Artists from Alberta:
Art in this Region.* London, England: Canada
House Cultural Centre and Edmonton, AB:
Alberta Culture, 1984

Varga, Vince. "Don Kottmann: The Odyssey."
Vanguard, 14(8) (October 1985) pp. 45-46

Caron, Quentin. "Painter's Abstracts Turn Toward
Figuration." *Calgary Herald,* April 13, 1984

Anonymous. "Don Kottmann." *Visual Arts
Newsletter,* 6(3) (June 1984)

Laviolette, Mary-Beth. "Don Kottmann -
New Paintings." *Vanguard,*
6(3) (May 1983) pp. 36-37

Tousley, Nancy. "Exhibition Prompts Praise for
City Gallery." *Calgary Herald,* February 10, 1983

Don Kottmann teaches at the Alberta College of
Art.

WILLIAM WALTER MACDONNELL

BORN:
1943, Winnipeg

EDUCATION:
1966
BSc, University of Manitoba

1977
BFA (Honours), University of Manitoba

1979
MFA, Nova Scotia College of Art and Design,
Halifax

SELECTED EXHIBITIONS:
Group
The Un-College Show, James Ulrich
Gallery, Calgary

Solo
1980
Arthur Street Gallery, Winnipeg

1981
Approaches to Paint, Gallery Moos, Calgary

1983
Anna Leonowens Gallery, Halifax

Torbolton Oaks Gallery, Ottawa

Off Centre Centre, Calgary

1985
Stride Gallery, Calgary

SELECTED BIBLIOGRAPHY:
Tousley, Nancy. "Works turn simple objects into
memory keys." *Calgary Herald,*
November 15, 1985

————. "Calgary artist offers acrylic
show-and-tell." *Calgary Herald,*
April 16, 1983

BILLY J. McCARROLL

BORN:
1937, Santa Barbara, California

Education:
1967
BA, California State University, San Francisco

1969
MA, California State University, Humboldt

SELECTED EXHIBITIONS:
Group
1980
Southern Exposure, circulated by Alberta Culture

This End Up - Landscape Within Landscape,
circulated by Alberta Culture

1983
Recent Acquisitions, Glenbow Museum, Calgary

1984
Southern Alberta Art Gallery, Lethbridge

1986
Transference, Walter Phillips Gallery,
Banff, Alberta

Solo
1981
New Paintings, Southern Alberta Art Gallery,
Lethbridge

1983
Recent Work, Torbolton Oaks Gallery, Ottawa

1984
Recent Paintings and Prints, Off Centre Centre,
Calgary

1986
*How to Play a Winning Game Your Natural Way:
The Metaphor Continues,* Dunlop Art Gallery,
Saskatoon

SELECTED BIBLIOGRAPHY:
Arnold, Grant. "Billy J. McCarroll." *Vanguard,*
3(4) (September 1986) pp. 42-43

Anonymous. "Mister Tee." *Canadian Art,*
3(3) (Fall/September 1986) pp. 23-24

White, Peter. *How to Play a Winning Game your
Natural Way: The Metaphor Continues.*
Regina, SK: Dunlop Art Gallery, 1986

Billy McCarroll is the chairman of the Art
Department at the University of Lethbridge.

CARROLL MOPPETT

BORN:
1948, Calgary

EDUCATION:
1966-67
Alberta College of Art, Calgary

1968
Instituto de Allende, Mexico

1974-75
Alberta College of Art, Calgary

SELECTED EXHIBITIONS:
Group
1980
Glen Guillett and Carroll Moppett, SUB Gallery
University of Alberta, Edmonton

Alberta Now, The Edmonton Art Gallery

Some Drawings by Some Albertans,
Alberta College of Art Gallery, Calgary

Mostly Smaller Works, Off Centre Centre, Calgary

1981
Ritual, The Winnipeg Perspective,
Winnipeg Art Gallery

1983
Studio Survey - Sculpture, Latitude 53, Edmonton

Drawing: A Canadian Survey 1977-1982,
touring exhibition, Saidye Bronfman Centre,
Montreal

1984
Seven Artists From Alberta: Art in this Region,
International touring exhibition: Canada House,
London, England; Canadian Cultural Centre,
Brussels, Belgium; Canadian Culture Centre,
Paris, France

Enigma, Alberta Invitational 1984, The Nickel
Arts Museum, Calgary

1985
*Contemporary Canadian Art from the
Canada Council Art Bank Collection,* Brockville
Arts Centre, Brockville, Ontario

1986
Convergence of Metamorphoses, Walter Phillips
Gallery, Banff, Alberta

Solo

1981
Carroll Moppett Sculpture and Drawings,
Glenbow Museum, Calgary; University of
Lethbridge Art Gallery; Mendel Art Gallery,
Saskatoon

1984
*Investigating Space: Sculpture and Drawings by
Carroll Moppett,* Southern Alberta Art Gallery,
Lethbridge

1986
Stride Gallery, Calgary

Anna Leonowens Gallery, Halifax

SELECTED BIBLIOGRAPHY:

Tousley, Nancy. "Roots, Rejections and Rewards in
Calgary." *Canadian Art,* 3(16) (Fall/September
1986) pp. 72-79

————. "Synthesis of experiences embraced."
Calgary Herald, March 14, 1986

————. "Exhibition cleverly pairs contrasting
styles." *Calgary Herald,* January 24, 1986

————. *Seven Artists from Alberta: Art
in this Region.* London, England:
Canada House Cultural Centre and
Edmonton, AB: Alberta Culture, 1984

————. "Carroll Moppett Sculpture and
Drawings." *Parachute,* (Winter Issue 1981)
pp. 26-27

Wilkins, Charles. "Rituals, Winnipeg Art Gallery."
Vanguard, 10(5/6) (Summer 1981) p. 48

Cochran, Bente. "Alberta: 75th Anniversary."
artmagazine, 12(53/54) (May/June 1981)
pp. 71-73

Enright, Robert. "Proch's 'visual pun' reflects
strengths of art gallery show."
Winnipeg Free Press, April 4, 1981

Tousley, Nancy. "In and out of the local galleries."
Calgary Herald, March 5, 1981

Allen, Karyn. "Criss-Crossing the Boundaries."
Ritual, The Winnipeg Perspective 1981.
Winnipeg, MAN: The Winnipeg Art Gallery, 1981

Tousley, Nancy. "Exhibition shows diversity of
drawing being done in Alberta." *Calgary Herald,*
November 27, 1980

RON MOPPETT

BORN:
1945, Woking, Surrey, England

EDUCATION:
1963-67
Alberta College of Art, Calgary

1968
Instituto de Allende, Mexico

SELECTED EXHIBITIONS:
Group
1980
Alberta Now, The Edmonton Art Gallery

Present Tense, Beaver House Gallery, Edmonton

Rose Museum (an exhibition), Off Centre Centre,
Calgary

Some Drawings by Some Albertans,
Alberta College of Art Gallery, Calgary

From Canada, Canadian Consulates in Atlanta,
Boston and Chicago

1981
Contemporary Alberta Art,
Glenbow Museum, Calgary

Art Across Canada, Harbourfront Art Gallery,
Toronto

Graphex 8, (invitational section), Art Gallery
of Brant, Brantford, Ontario

*Jeff Spalding, John Will, Ron Moppett: Recent
Paintings,* University of Lethbridge Art Gallery

1982
Curnoe/Ewen/Falk/Moppett, Norman Mackenzie
Art Gallery, Regina and Nickle Arts Museum,
University of Calgary

Gallery 111, University of Manitoba, Winnipeg

1983
Ten: 83, Beaver House Gallery, Edmonton

*The Hand Holding the Brush, Self Portraits by
Canadian Artists,* national touring exhibition,
organized by the London Regional Art Gallery

1984
Edge and Image, Concordia Art Gallery, Montreal

Seven Artists From Alberta: Art in this Region,
international touring exhibition: Canada House,
London, England; Canadian Cultural Centre,
Brussels, Belgium; Canadian Cultural Centre,
Paris, France

Now Showing in Europe, Beaver House Gallery,
Edmonton

Canada Council Art Bank Show, Charles H. Scott
Gallery, Emily Carr College of Art, Vancouver

*Reflections, Contemporary Art Since 1964
at the National Gallery of Canada,*
National Gallery, Ottawa

1985
The First Ten, Off Centre Centre, Calgary

1986
Looking at Myself, Off Centre Centre, Calgary

1986-87
Eighth Dalhousie Drawing Exhibition,
national touring exhibition, organized by
Dalhousie University, Halifax

Solo
1981
SUB Art Gallery, University of Alberta, Edmonton

1982
Walter Phillips Gallery, Banff, Alberta

Ron Moppett exhibits regularly at Paul Kuhn Fine
Art, Calgary and Mira Godard Gallery, Toronto.

SELECTED BIBLIOGRAPHY:

Tousley, Nancy. "Artist Looks Both Inward and
Out." *Calgary Herald,* November 7, 1986

————. "Roots, Rejections and Rewards in
Calgary."
Canadian Art, 3(16) (Fall/September 1986)
pp. 72-79

————. "Painter Adds Air in Studio."
Calgary Herald, June 8, 1986

Tivy, Patrick. "Society Helps to Feed Glenbow
Culture Machine." *Calgary Herald,*
January 29, 1986

Tousley, Nancy. "Couple's Work Reflect Creative
Dialogue." *Calgary Herald,* November 3, 1983

Murray, Joan. "The Season in Review: Toronto,
Ron Moppett at Mira Godard Gallery."
Art Magazine, 14(63) (Summer 1983) p. 48

Tousley, Nancy. "Moppett Display Reveals a
Significant Breakthrough." *Calgary Herald,*
October 14, 1982

Howse, John. "Albertan Brings Wild World of Art
to Banff." *Calgary Herald,* July 3, 1982

McDougall, Arthur. "Show at U. of L. Arts Centre
Displays Trivia, Some Richness." *The Lethbridge
Herald,* September 30, 1981

BRUCE O'NEIL

BORN:
1942, Winnipeg

EDUCATION:
1961-64
Alberta College of Art, Calgary
1965
Instituto de Allende, Mexico

SELECTED EXHIBITIONS:
Group
1980
Alberta '75, The Edmonton Art Gallery

Recent Acquisitions, Glenbow-Alberta Institute, Calgary

1982
Canadian Horizons, Paintings from the Canada Council, Fairbanks; Anchorage; Juneau, Alaska

1986
3 x 3 Show, Off Centre Centre, Calgary

Bruce O'Neil exhibits regularly at Canadian Art Galleries, Calgary.

SELECTED BIBLIOGRAPHY:
Joyner, Brooks. "O'Neil Exhibit Tackles Problem." *The Albertan,* March 2, 1980

Tousley, Nancy. "Visual Arts." *Calgary Herald,* February 7, 1980

Bruce O'Neil teaches at the University of Calgary.

MARY ELIZABETH SCOTT

BORN:
1948, Calgary

EDUCATION:
1974-78
BFA, University of Calgary
1978-80
MFA, Nova Scotia College of Art and Design, Halifax

SELECTED EXHIBITIONS:
Group
1980
Alberta Now, The Edmonton Art Gallery

University of New Mexico, Albuquerque

1983
Connection, Martin Gerard Gallery, Edmonton

1984
Seven Artists from Alberta: Art in This Region
International touring exhibition: Canada House, London, England; Canadian Cultural Centre, Brussels, Belgium; Canadian Cultural Centre, Paris, France

1985
She Writes in White Ink, Walter Phillips Gallery, Banff, Alberta

5 x 5 Show, Off Centre Centre, Calgary

1986
Words, Off Centre Centre, Calgary

Politically Speaking, Latitude 53, Edmonton

Songs of Experience, National Gallery, Ottawa

Solo
1980-81
Glenbow Museum, Calgary

1981
Southern Alberta Art Gallery, Lethbridge

1983
University of Lethbridge Art Gallery

1985
Marking Out: Recent Work, Whyte Museum of the Canadian Rockies, Banff, Alberta

1986
Paintings 1978-1985, Dunlop Art Gallery, Regina
travelling exhibition: Mendel Art Gallery, Saskatoon; Dalhousie Art Gallery, Halifax; Powerhouse, Montreal

SELECTED BIBLIOGRAPHY:
Tousley, Nancy. "Roots, Rejections and Rewards in Calgary." *Canadian Art,* 3(16) (September 1986) pp. 72-79

————. "Scott's Rug Size Work Takes Over Living Room." *Calgary Herald,* March 2, 1986

Anonymous. "Mary Scott." *Visual Arts Newsletter,* 6(3) (June 1984)

Shaw, Sanora. "Future Selected Exhibitions." *Update,* 6 (November/December 1981) (Edmonton Art Gallery)

Tousley, Nancy. "Striking Originality Animates the Work of Calgary Artist." *Calgary Herald,* January 29, 1981

Mary Scott teaches painting and drawing at the Alberta College of Art, Calgary.

ROBERT AUSTIN SCOTT

BORN:
1941, Melfort, Saskatchewan

EDUCATION:
1969
Diploma of Applied Arts, Alberta College of Art, Calgary

1973
Michael Steiner Workshop,
The Edmonton Art Gallery

1976
MVA, University of Alberta, Edmonton

1982
Triangle Artist's Workshop, Pine Plains, New York

SELECTED EXHIBITIONS:
Group
1980
Alberta Now, The Edmonton Art Gallery

A Glimpse of the Present, touring exhibition,
Cultural Development Branch, Alberta

Alberta Art, Shell Gallery, Calgary

1981
Modernist Painting and Sculpture,
Glenbow Museum, Calgary

Abstract an Narration: Recent Tendencies in Canadian Painting, Shell Gallery, Calgary

1982
Triangle Workshop Exhibition,
Pine Plains, New York

Westburne Collection, The Edmonton Art Gallery

1983
My Favorite Picture, The Edmonton Art Gallery

1984
The Sixtieth Anniversary Exhibition,
The Edmonton Art Gallery

Studio Watch, The Edmonton Art Gallery

Solo
1980
Recent Paintings, Gallery Moos, Calgary

1981
New Works, Gallery One, Toronto

1982
New Painting, Gallery Moos, Calgary

1985
Gallery Moos, Toronto

Robert Scott has also exhibited at Gallery Moos, Toronto; Gallery One, Toronto and the Martin Gerard Gallery, Edmonton

SELECTED BIBLIOGRAPHY:
Bingham, Russell. "Paintings of the '80's." *Update,* 7(1) (January/February 1986) pp. 5-6 (Edmonton Art Gallery)

JEFFREY SPALDING

BORN:
1951, Edinburgh, Scotland

EDUCATION:
1973
BA (Fine Art), University of Guelph

1975
MA (Art Education), Ohio State University, Columbus, Ohio

1976
MFA, Nova Scotia College of Art and Design, Halifax

SELECTED EXHIBITIONS:
Group
1981
John Will, Ron Moppett, Jeffrey Spalding,
University of Lethbridge Art Gallery

1982
Galerie Anne Doran, Ottawa

Susan Whitney Gallery, Regina

New Image Alberta, touring exhibition organized by the Alberta College of Art

Art as a Commodity, Exhibition Centre, Castlegar, B.C.

1983
The Miniature Art Show, London Regional Art Gallery, London, Ontario

The Banff Retrospective Exhibition, Banff, Alberta

1984
The Tower Show, Off Centre Centre, Calgary

Seven Artists from Alberta: Art in this Region touring exhibition, Canada House, London, England; Canadian Cultural Centre, Brussels, Belgium; Canadian Cultural Centre, Paris, France

Images: New Representational Art,
The Edmonton Art Gallery

Now Showing in Europe, Beaver House Gallery, Edmonton

Artist's Choice: Six New Faces, Glendon Art Gallery, York University, Toronto

Contemporary Art in Southern Alberta (a selection), Off Centre Centre, Calgary

1985
Canada Council Art Bank, Selections,
College Park Gallery, Toronto

74

1986
The Romantic Landscape Now, touring exhibition
organized by Artspace, Peterborough, Ontario

Culture's Nature: Douglas Kirton,
David Thauberger Gerald Fergusson,
Jeffrey Spalding, Dunlop Art Gallery, Regina

1987
Douglas Kirton, Jeffrey Spalding, 49th Parallel
Centre for Canadian Art, New York

Solo
1980
Drawings, Agnes Etherington Art Gallery,
Queen's University, Kingston

1981
Recent Paintings, Mendel Art Gallery, Saskatoon

Jeffrey Spalding, SUB Art Gallery, University
of Alberta, Edmonton

1982
The Black Paintings, The Southern Alberta Art
Gallery, Lethbridge

Galerie Anne Doran, Ottawa

1983
James Ulrich Gallery, Calgary

1984
Art Gallery of Greater Victoria

1985
Canadian Art Galleries, Calgary

Jeffrey Spalding exhibits regularly at the
Waddington/Shiell Gallery, Toronto and
Canadian Art Galleries, Calgary.

SELECTED BIBLIOGRAPHY:
Tousley, Nancy. "Artist Enters New Phase."
Calgary Herald, March 15, 1985

————. "Tower Show Lets Fantasy Road Freely."
Calgary Herald, July 6, 1984

Anonymous. "Jeffrey Spalding." *Visual Arts*
Newsletter, 6(3) (June 1984)

McDougall, Arthur. "Show At U. of L. Arts Centre
Displays Trivia, Some Richness."
The Lethbridge Herald, September 30, 1981

Tousley, Nancy. "Edgy Tension Links Widely
Different Works." *Calgary Herald,*
September 15, 1983

Anonymous. "Salon-Style Display Method Sets
Off Show." *Calgary Herald,* June 11, 1981

Jeffrey Spalding is the Director of the University
of Lethbridge Art Gallery.

SUZANNE SPIEGEL-BELL

BORN:
1952, Toronto, Ontario

EDUCATION:
1978
BFA, York University, Toronto

1983
MVA, University of Alberta, Edmonton

SELECTED EXHIBITIONS:
1980
Ontario Institute for Studies in Education, Toronto

1983
Vik Gallery, Edmonton

1985
The Edmonton Art Gallery

Robert Vanderleelie Gallery, Edmonton,

Suzanne Spiegel-Bell teaches at the University of
Alberta, Edmonton.

DAVID VERCHOMIN

BORN:
1959, Edmonton

EDUCATION:
1981
BFA, University of Alberta, Edmonton

1984
MFA, Maryland Institute, College of Art,
Baltimore

SELECTED EXHIBITIONS:
Group
1984
Aspects of People, Multicultural Heritage Centre,
Stony Plain, Alberta

1985
Points North, Southern Alberta Art Gallery,
Lethbridge

Discoveries, Latitude 53 Gallery,
Edmonton

1986
The Human Image, a segment of *The Works,*
Manulife Place, Edmonton

David Verchomin teaches at the University of
Alberta, Edmonton.

JOHN WILL

BORN:
1939, Waterloo, Iowa,

EDUCATION:
1961
BA, University of Northern Iowa
1964
MFA, University of Iowa
1964-65
Fulbright Fellow, Amsterdam
1970-71
Ford Foundation Fellow, Tamarind Institute

SELECTED EXHIBITIONS:
Group
1980
Canadian Biennale of Prints and Drawings,
The Edmonton Art Gallery

Gravures de l'ouest, Montreal

A.F.N. Print Exhibition, University of Toronto

On/Of Paper, Visual Center of Alaska, Anchorage
1981
Graphics 8, Art Gallery of Brant,
Brantford, Ontario

Harbourfront Gallery, Toronto

Abstraction and Narration,
Shell Gallery, Calgary

This End Up, The Edmonton Art Gallery

University of Lethbridge Art Gallery
1982
Dunlop Art Gallery, Regina

Winnipeg Art Gallery, Winnipeg

Graphica Gallery, Edmonton
1983
The Edmonton Art Gallery

20s Show, Portico Gallery, Philadelphia

Locations, Off Centre Centre, Calgary
1984
Seven Artists from Alberta: Art in this Region,
touring exhibition: Canada House London,
England; Canadian Cultural Centre, Brussels,
Belgium; Canadian Cultural Centre, Paris France,
Bury Art Galleries, England

Tenth Anniversary Show, Off Centre Centre,
Calgary

Currents, Off Centre Centre, Calgary

1985
Nicle Arts Museum, Calgary
(*ICON I* with Jack Anderson)

10th Anniversary Show, Off Centre Centre,
Calgary (*ICON II,* with Jack Anderson)

ICON III, (with Jack Anderson), Kamloops Public
Art Gallery

Whirly-Gig, Alberta College of Art,
Calgary, (*ICON IV* with Jack Anderson)

Kanadensisk Grafik, Sveagalleriet, Stockholm,
Sweden

Anxiety, Alienation, Aphasia, University of
Lethbridge Art Gallery
1986
Albertasta, Galleria Harmonia, Jyvaskyla,
Sweden

Alberta Art and Artist, University of Lethbridge

Nickle Arts Museum, Calgary
(*ICON V* with Jack Anderson)

Solo
1980
Glenbow Museum, Calgary

Gallery Moos, Calgary
1981
Anna Leonowens Gallery, Halifax

Southern Alberta Art Gallery, Lethbridge

London Regional Art Gallery, London, Ontario
1982
Mendel Art Gallery, Saskatoon

Art Gallery of Greater Victoria
1984
Anna Leonowens Gallery, Halifax

University of Wisconsin-Stout,
Menomonie, Wisconsin
1986
Stride Gallery, Calgary

SELECTED BIBLIOGRAPHY:
Tousley, Nancy. "Roots, Rejections and Rewards in
Calgary." *Canadian Art,* 3(16)
(Fall/September 1986) pp. 72-79

Blanchette Manon. "John Will Oeuvre Sur La
Banalite Historique." *Vie Des Arts,* (June 1986)
pp. 80-81

Tousley, Nancy. "Friends and Graves." *Vanguard,*
(April/May 1986) pp. 34-36.

————. "Artist enters a dialogue with
photography." *Calgary Herald,* January 10, 1986

Greenfield, Valerie. *The Wild West: A Vision
Within Canadian Borders.* 3rd Annual Wild West
Show, Calgary, AB: Alberta College of Art Gallery

Laviolette, Mary-Beth. "Currents." *Vanguard,*
13(4) (May 1984) p. 39

Tousley, Nancy. *Seven Artists from Alberta:
Art in this Region.* London, England: Canada
House Cultural Centre and Edmonton, AB:
Alberta Culture, 1984

————. "Artists Turn On Power in Currents."
Calgary Herald, February 19, 1984.

Nowosad, Frank. "John Will Retrospective."
Art Magazine, (December 1981) pp. 62-63

Spalding, Jeffrey. *John Will.*
Calgary, AB: Glenbow Museum, 1980

Tousley, Nancy. "Humorous Calgary lithographer
sends witty darts into local art scene."
Calgary Herald, January 10, 1980

John Will teaches art at the University of Calgary.

All dimensions are given in inches; height precedes width.

1. GIUSEPPE ALBI
OR-AR, 1986
acrylic on canvas
58.8 x 56.8"
Courtesy of Woltjen/Udell Gallery, Edmonton

2. GIUSEPPE ALBI
BERG, 1986
acrylic on canvas
72.8 x 36"
Courtesy of Woltjen/Udell Gallery, Edmonton

3. JACK ANDERSON
The Conversation, 1985
lacquer on plastic laminate
19.5 x 19.5"
Collection of John Will

4. JACK ANDERSON
Growling at the Moon, 1985
acrylic on canvas
30 x 30"
Collection of Glenbow Museum
Purchased 1987 with funds from the
Glenbow Museum Acquisitions Society

5. JOHN BROCKE
Barb/Barbaros, 1985
oil on canvas
60 x 144"
Collection of Glenbow Museum
Purchased 1986 with funds from the
Glenbow Museum Acquisitions Society

6. JOHN BROCKE
Untitled, 1986
oil on canvas
60 x 144"
Collection of Mr. and Mrs. Philip B. Lind, Toronto

7. CHRIS CRAN
*Self Portrait Watching a Man
About to Shoot Himself in the Foot*, 1984
oil on canvas
60 x 84"
Collection of Glenbow Museum
Purchased 1986 with funds from the
Glenbow Museum Acquisitions Society

8. CHRIS CRAN
Self Portrait as Max Beckman, 1986
oil on canvas
55.4 x 38.4"
Collection: The University of Calgary
at The Nickle Arts Museum

9. EVA DIENER
Toxic # 10, 1986
acrylic on canvas
67.2 x 102.8"
Collection of the artist

10. EVA DIENER
Toxic # 12 , 1987
acrylic on canvas
80 x 160"
Collection of the artist

11. ALAN DUNNING
Unfinished Business - Seaside, 1986-87
mixed media
144 x 177"
Collection of the artist

12. ALAN DUNNING
Unfinished Business - Skin, 1986
oil, enamel and gold leaf on arborite,
gravel on wood
two panels, 31 x 31"
Collection of the artist

13. WAYNE GILES
No Picnic, 1986
acrylic on canvas
86 x 65"
Collection of the artist

14. WAYNE GILES
Race, 1986
acrylic on canvas
90 x 65"
Collection of the Canada Council Art Bank

15. JOHN HALL
Arlene, 1986
acrylic on canvas
60 x 60"
Private collection, Toronto
Courtesy of Wynick/Tuck Gallery, Toronto

16. JOHN HALL
Indigo, 1986
acrylic on canvas
60 x 60"
Courtesy of Wynick/Tuck Gallery, Toronto

17. JOICE HALL
Floating (panels 11, 12, 13 & 14)
oil on canvas
72 x 192"
Collection of the artist

18. DOUG HAYNES
Apple Swing, 1986
acrylic on canvas
64.75 x 25.5"
Collection of Ellen Thompson and Al Reynolds

19. DOUG HAYNES
Diego's Table, 1986
acrylic on canvas
67 x 25.25"
Collection of the artist

20. GERALD HUSHLAK
Untitled, 1986-87
oil on canvas, (three modules)
90 x 180"
Collection of the artist

CATALOGUE OF THE EXHIBITION

21. GERALD HUSHLAK
I asked for horse shoes, they gave me wings.
Now I'm going to fly!, 1986-87
oil on canvas, (four modules)
138 x 192"
Collection of the artist

22. TERRENCE KELLER
Hat Med, 1985-86
acrylic, gel on canvas
52 x 148.5"
Collection of the artist

23. TERRENCE KELLER
Round Midnight, 1987
acrylic on canvas
54 x 119.5"
Collection of the artist

24. DON KOTTMANN
Last Judgement, 1986
acrylic on canvas
139.5 x 115.75"
Collection of the artist

25. DON KOTTMANN
Beacon Tandava, 1986
acrylic on canvas
71 x 190.5"
Collection of the artist

26. WILLIAM MACDONNELL
Untitled, 1985
oil on canvas
60 x 120"
Collection of Glenbow Museum
Purchased 1986 with funds from the
Glenbow Museum Acquisitions Society

27. WILLIAM MACDONNELL
Untitled, 1985
oil on canvas
18 x 18"
Collection of John Will

28. BILLY McCARROLL
Full Follow Through, 1986
oil stick and oil on canvas
64.6 x 64.6"
Collection of the Alberta Art Foundation

29. BILLY McCARROLL
The Square Stance, 1986
oil on canvas
80.3 x 59.9"
Collection of Glenbow Museum
Purchased 1987 with funds from the
Glenbow Museum Acquisitions Society

30. CARROLL MOPPETT
Like Trying to See Beograd, #2, 1985
oil on canvas
96 x 66"
Courtesy of the Wynick/Tuck Gallery, Toronto

31. CARROLL MOPPETT
Biography, Autobiography: I am I Not Any
Longer When I See, 1985
charcoal on canvas
66.5 x 210"
Collection of Glenbow Museum
Purchased 1985 with funds from the
Glenbow Museum Acquisitions Society

32. RON MOPPETT
Oenone 1986-87
oil, mixed media on canvas
106 x 307" (overall)
Collection of the artist

33. RON MOPPETT
Indian Red/Portrait/Buffalo, 1983
oil on canvas, teddy bear, wood
72.8 x 64.8"
Collection of Glenbow Museum
Purchased 1984 with the assistance of
Shell Canada

34. BRUCE O'NEIL
Tenak, 1986
acrylic on canvas
50 x 85"
Collection of the artist

35. BRUCE O'NEIL
Silver Shift, 1980-84
acrylic on canvas
55 x 77"
David Duffin Collection, DeWinton, Alberta

36. MARY SCOTT
Untitled (quoting L. Irigaray, R. Barthes;
image - Jean Genet, 1953), 1986
mixed media
72 x 100"
Collection of the artist

37. MARY SCOTT
Untitled (Stealers!), 1986
mixed media, (diptych)
1 panel 72 x 104", 1 panel 72 x 76"
Collection of the artist

38. ROBERT SCOTT
Graphite Whisper, 1986
acrylic on canvas
83.5 x 140"
Private collection

39. ROBERT SCOTT
Tanbooma, 1987
acrylic on canvas
91 x 43.5"
Sharecom Collection

40. JEFF SPALDING
Nightfall, 1984-85
oil on canvas
79.5 x 158"
Collection of the Alberta Art Foundation

41. JEFF SPALDING
Dark Source: Threshold, 1987
oil on canvas
96 x 66"
Courtesy of Waddington and Shiell
Gallery, Toronto

42. SUZANNE SPIEGEL-BELL
C Player, 1986-87
acrylic on canvas
73 x 66"
Collection of the artist

43. SUZANNE SPIEGEL-BELL
Edison Waits, 1986-87
acrylic on canvas
73 x 66"
Collection of the artist

44. DAVID VERCHOMIN
Picture of Friday, 1986
oil on canvas
65 x 53.5"
Collection of the artist

45. DAVID VERCHOMIN
Window Pie 1, 1986
oil on canvas
39 x 30"
Collection of the artist

46. JOHN WILL
Untitled, 1985
oil on canvas
88 x 68"
Collection of the artist

47. JOHN WILL
Untitled, 1983
oil on canvas
88 x 68"
Collection of the artist

Giuseppe Albi 20, 64

Jack Anderson 26, 64

John Brocke 28, 65

Chris Cran 30, 65

Eva Diener 14, 65

Alan Dunning 32, 66

Wayne Giles 34, 66

John Hall 36, 67

Joice Hall 38, 68

Doug Haynes 16, 68

Gerald Hushlak 40, 69

Terry Keller 18, 69

Don Kottmann 42, 70

William MacDonnell 44, 71

Billy J. McCarroll 56, 71

Carroll Moppett 46, 71

Ron Moppett 48, 72

Bruce O'Neil 50, 73

Mary Scott 52, 73

Robert Scott 20, 74

Jeffrey Spalding 58, 74

Suzanne Spiegel-Bell 22, 75

David Verchomin 24, 75

John Will 54, 76

INDEX OF ARTISTS

Giuseppe Albi,   Edmonton
Eva Diener,   Edmonton
David Duffin,   DeWinton
Alan Dunning,   Calgary
Wayne Giles,   Calgary
John Hall,   Calgary
Joice Hall,   Calgary
Douglas Haynes,   Edmonton
Gerald Hushlak,   Calgary
Terry Keller,   Edmonton
Don Kottmann,   Calgary
Mr. and Mrs. Philip B. Lind,   Toronto
Carroll Moppett,   Calgary
Ron Moppett,   Calgary
Bruce O'Neil,   Calgary
Mary Scott,   Calgary
Robert Scott,   Edmonton
Jeffrey Spalding,   Bobcaygeon, Ontario
Suzanne Spiegel-Bell,   Edmonton
Ellen Thompson and Al Reynolds,   Edmonton
David Verchomin,   Edmonton
John Will,   Calgary

The Alberta Art Foundation,   Edmonton
Canada Council Art Bank,   Ottawa
The Nickle Arts Museum,   University of Calgary
Sharecom Limited,   Edmonton
Waddington/Shiell Gallery,   Toronto
Woltjen/Udell Gallery,   Edmonton
Wynick/Tuck Gallery,   Toronto

LENDERS TO THE EXHIBITION

Design: Nelson Vigneault

Editor: Elise L. Wittig

Typesetting: Paperwords

Printing: Paperworks Press Limited, Calgary

Binding: Atlas Book Binding, Edmonton

Photography: Ron Marsh, Glenbow Museum
Tom Moore, Toronto (*Indigo* and *NightFall*)

CREDITS